The Vanishing Kingdom

A memoir of Swaziland
by Edith Hall
Copyright 2019 by Edith Hall
Cover design by Adrienne Kern

The past is another country

On the occasion of his 50th birthday in 2018 King Mswati III, the last remaining absolute monarch in sub Saharan Africa, gave the country of Swaziland a surprise present. Previous presents he had given himself included a second private jet at an estimated (secret) cost of US$30 million, a suit heavily encrusted with diamonds weighing 6kg, a watch worth US$1.6 million and a fifty tier birthday cake it had taken 4 months to make.

His present to his people wasn't food for the starving; it wasn't land for the landless or medicines for the empty shelves of hospitals, jobs for the 40% unemployed or the restoration of pensions for the old. It was a new name for the country. From now on it would be called eSwatini and Swaziland would be no more. And this new country wouldn't even, officially, start with a capital, only a small e. As absolute monarch, Mswati didn't need to consult his parliament or his people about this decision. He could imprison people, order their assassination, take over their land and businesses, send his soldiers to "escort" a young girl from school to be his latest wife, fine people or demand vast sums of money; he could order major building works at whim, decide what his subjects can and cannot read in newspapers, on their iphones, hear on the radio or see on TV, what can be reported or photographed. He was above the law, could not be questioned and his commands had to be obeyed. The second smallest country on the continent of Africa, only 109 miles from north to south and 83 miles from east to west, sandwiched between South Africa and Mozambique, Swaziland is, or was, a beautiful little gem of a country. It is of no strategic interest and largely overlooked by most countries of the world but it now has a humanitarian crisis which the world should know about. The plight of Swazi women is particularly concerning. Even the king's wives are possessions. They have the status of children and are unable, under Swazi law, to control their own lives. They are dealt with largely as their menfolk please, needing their permission to have a bank account, a passport, hospital or doctor visits, to enrol for higher education, to own property and to earn money. What they wear or even, in extreme cases, just going out also requires permission. Even the right to farm any Swazi Nation land is granted by chiefs only to male heads of households. Yet the women of Swaziland are the glue that holds the nation together. They have remarkable endurance and resilience but they have no voice, so we need to tell their story.

When I first encountered Swaziland all those years ago, I found a country of laid back, friendly people who loved to dance and sing. The old king had just died after a much respected leadership of more than sixty years and the present king was a schoolboy in England. Mandela was still in prison, apartheid and sanctions were in full swing in South Africa next door. A communist revolution was simmering in Mozambique on the other side. Amongst all this, the Swazi nation was peaceful, largely crime free and prosperous and for me, a life changing discovery. So what went wrong?

A new start

I knew I was going to like Swaziland as soon as I found the Ministry of Education housed, temporarily it must be owned, above a butcher's shop in the shopping plaza of the capital Mbabane.

It was an urgent appointment, I was told by the Overseas Development Administration. I should be ready to leave in a month so I handed in my notice and bustled around getting myself and my son, David, ready. Then all I had to do was wait for the call to get on the plane.

And I waited and waited. Just a slight hitch, ODA kept assuring me. Don't panic. The news, when it eventually reached me, that the brand new Ngwane Teacher Training College, the flagship of EEC aid, was at that moment a mere ten bricks high, would have put paid to the whole enterprise had I not already burnt my boats. Weeks of postponement for this "urgent post" turned into months. I was becoming more and more convinced that I had made a disastrous mistake. Five months of unpaid unemployment followed. Things were not looking good.

"Please hang on," ODA kept begging me as though I had any choice at that point.

They sent me to Farnham Castle, the International Briefing Centre, for the weekend just, I suspect, to keep me on the boil. They even found two real Swazis to come and meet me there to talk about their country. They were two young soldiers training at nearby Sandhurst and, since their command of English was very sketchy and I was the only ODA candidate there scheduled to go to Swaziland, it was very hard work to keep up a conversation all evening.

"What is it that you do for the king back home?" I asked casually, just for something else to say.

"We dance," they said.

It conjured up a delightful picture but it couldn't possibly be true, could it? But it could, as I was to find out. Well, sort of. Not in their khaki serge and hobnailed boots as members of the National Defence Force but in their other, their real Swazi role, as the king's own warriors, bare chested, waving their spears and knobkerries while dancing and stamping out the rhythm of the drums with their bare feet. They might have added, "And we guard the royal family, help the age regiments weed the king's lands and kill the black bull at the time of the Incwala". What they seemed not to do, at that point anyway, unlike many other African countries, was to get involved in tribal warfare or fighting of any sort for that matter. But then, they had no need to. The Swazis were one tribe, one kingdom, one tiny country crooked in an elbow of the Republic of

6

South Africa and bounded on the eastern, seaward side by Mozambique; both troubled and troublesome neighbours at that time in the early eighties with whom it was important to stay on good terms. When the British had charge of the Protectorate till independence in 1968, Swaziland had no army at all apart, that is, from the traditional impi age regiments which were entirely in the hands of the king. Civil order was the responsibility of the colonial police and any threat from the two neighbours would be so overwhelming, thought the British, that keeping an expensive army would be a complete waste of scarce resources. If needed, troops could always be flown in from other parts of Africa as happened in 1963 when 300 Gordon Highlanders arrived to quell what almost became a general strike. But more of that later.

It was just around Christmas time when David and I actually took off. This had better be worth it, I thought. After my previous experience in Kenya as a single parent with a child when I was forced to spend three weeks in a hotel room next door to the "Paradise Massage Parlour, we aim to please" both of which, the aiming and pleasing, they did busily and noisily, I thought I had better go in advance this time and not expose my son to a further dose of inadvertent sex education. Not that it had escaped him the previous time.

"It's the local cat house next door," my (then) eleven

year old informed me in case his mother hadn't worked it out for herself.

This time, I decided, I would leave him with friends in Nairobi while I went ahead to settle us in.

The stay in Mbabane, the capital, was mercifully short; just long enough to be put on the High Commission's list of emergency evacuees and as a potential recipient, amongst other things, of clean needles and good uncontaminated British blood (whatever that might be) should the need arise. Rather disappointingly, I wasn't actually given a phial of pure British blood to carry around with me, or clean needles. They were kept together with an emergency medical kit and special evacuation instructions in the safe keeping of someone appointed for that task. Luckily, we were never called upon to evacuate. That would have proved somewhat tricky anyway since the country only had one smallish airport and a Fokker Friendship aircraft which was high-jacked at one point and used to stage an abortive coup in the Seychelles. When it was eventually recovered there were several large bullet holes in the fuselage and it had to be sent back to Holland for repairs. But I digress.

The Ministry over the butcher's shop laid on a Combi to take me down to the south of the country to Nhlangano, which was to be my home, as it turned out, not for three but for the next six years. When I first applied for the post with ODA, I couldn't find Nhlangano in my old school atlas. It was hard enough to find Swaziland. Nhlangano; near the South African border the advertisement had said. Given the size of the country, everything was near the South African border. The explanation, they told me, was quite simple really; they'd changed the name from the Afrikaans Goetgegun after Independence and my atlas hadn't caught up. I'd rather fancied the thought of travelling to a place that had no official existence for the rest of the world.

I could almost imagine we really were heading for some uncharted destination when we set off in the Combi. We travelled down a tarmaced road through the appropriately named beautiful Valley of Heaven, past the equally appropriately named Execution Rock and eventually turned on to a dirt road.

"They are building a beautiful new road through this valley," said the Swazi driver with pride as we came to it, "Before we had to drive other way, long, long over the mountains to Shiselweni ... bad road ... plenty of punctures ... but now it will be fast."

Rather like my immediate, urgent appointment to the new college, this turned out to be a bit of wishful thinking. Time and again we were brought to a halt by bulldozers still shifting mountains of red soil or driving piles into river beds. Quite unfazed and grinning hugely, the driver would turn and detour up

9

through the rocky scrub of virgin hills, splash through rivers or very reluctantly acknowledge that he was driving a minibus and not a tractor and wait for a friendly bulldozer to arrive and compact the piles of soft, loose, top soil so we could continue. The adventurous journey obviously made his day and he took to the bush with a verve that swayed the vehicle dangerously from side to side, bounced me in my seat and had him laughing in delight. Cows, children, goats and dogs meandered over the road as though it wasn't there at all. Thatched, round clay and wattle huts clung to the hillsides chameleon like, blending into their surroundings, while the corrugated iron roofs of the more modern homes flashed and dazzled in the midday sun.

As we approached the distant mountains the sky began to blacken sending deep shadows over the peaks till all the colours were swallowed by a grey sky over black summits. And then I saw them, thousands of tiny white butterflies like pollen suddenly highlighted by the sombre backdrop, dancing in a mad frenzy before the storm.

"Just look at that! How exquisite!"

"Look at what?" said the driver, puzzled.

"All those wonderful white butterflies. So pretty."

"Very bad." was his verdict "They make many, many army worms and the harvest will be spoilt. Very bad…very bad," he kept muttering as he accelerated through the cloud of insects, more intent on doing his bit for the prospects of the next Swazi harvest by splattering them all across the windscreen than being able to see ahead and driving safely down a difficult road.

We hit the storm just as we got to the mountains. Lightning flashed between the peaks followed by rain and hail which thundered on the roof and scoured the windscreen clean of blood and wings. Through the solid curtain of water, I saw nothing of the landscape, not even the road in front. Just as well, I reflected many times later, when I drove the same route on clear days, nervously negotiating the sharp bends and sheer, unguarded drops. "What the eye doesn't see"… Even so, I was distinctly weak at the knees, staggering out at the college at the end of the four hour ordeal.

Much to my relief, there had been a considerable advance from the last report of unfinished buildings. Everything seemed to have a roof, including my little bungalow; water came out of the taps and light appeared when you switched on. The gardens were mere mounds of builders' rubble and the grounds bare of trees or even a blade of grass, but the views were spectacular. Dense eucalyptus and conifer plantations covered the surrounding hills scarred here and there with bare, rocky patches where a thin layer of red soil was all that remained after a section of mature trees had been harvested. After the rain, a faint scent like Vicks Vapour wafted across from the forest reminding me of childhood colds. Among the trees and meadows around all was silence apart from birdsong.

As soon as the combi pulled up, Mike Villeneuve came to welcome me with an offer of tea. I'd met him once briefly at the appointment session and once again at an ODA meeting with Dr Barnard. A rather reserved man possibly in his mid to late thirties, he'd been sent out earlier to help get the college administration off the ground. Remembering how stiffly he'd held himself at our previous meetings, how reluctant to let go even a tiny part of his private space, I was agreeably surprised. He even took the trouble to make me some "proper tea" while sticking to his own herbal brew.

"I was afraid you might have dropped out," he said conversationally, "like Gilbert Steine, the Science chap."

"Yes, I heard about that. Can't blame him, can you, with all this delay. I probably would have too if I'd known how long it would be to pay day. So what was all that about being so urgent?"

"You might well ask," Mike groaned, "What a nightmare that was. Typical Swazi shambles. They couldn't wait till everything was in place. The first thirty students turned up – no college! They didn't know what to do with them so they sent them out on what they called "prolonged teaching practice" staying in whatever local homesteads they could find for themselves. They were still out when I turned up three months later! To crown it all, in the panic, no one had thought to keep a record of where they were or whether they'd even arrived at any of the schools so we had to go out searching for them."

"No phones."

"Right. Nor electricity, most of them."

"So what happened?"

"Well, the High Commission lent us a clapped out old van and we took to the hills. No idea where the schools were located either! That was an added complication – that and the weather. You know how thick the mist can be in these mountains. Couldn't see a thing! Sometimes we just had to switch off the engine and all sit and listen for the sound of children chanting and follow the direction. But we found them all in the end and farmed the students out to the other colleges up north. It's a great life if you can survive the frustration."

"Well, I'm delighted to see that I have a roof over my head anyway. After all the horror stories I almost expected a mud hut. David will be relieved."

13

"Where is your son?"

"I left him with some friends in Nairobi while I sussed out the situation here. His school doesn't start for ten days anyway."

"So, you're on your own for New Year"

"Looks like it."

"I was … I was wondering if you'd like to see the New Year in with me? New country, new job and all that. We could have dinner at the Casino… I'm afraid it's the only place we've got locally," he ended with a rush.

"How very kind of you. I'd like that."

I was touched. For a vegetarian who didn't drink, disapproved of gambling and hated crowd bonhomie, it really was a huge sacrifice.

It was a sacrifice he was spared from making because the Casino was fully booked, chock-a-block with white and Indian South Africans who crossed the border if they wanted to gamble or associate with black girls, both forbidden in apartheid South Africa and a sufficient reason for Holiday Inns to establish a hotel and casino here in this rural backwater. It truly was the only hotel in town and one that would loom large in my life. So, on New Year's eve, Mike cooked some curried pumpkin with brown rice and we toasted the New Year in pineapple juice. No midnight chimes from Big Ben, no bright lights, only the blackness of the sudden African night, the silence pierced by unseen regiments of cicadas fiddling notes of shrill, unending monotony and the deep croak of frogs. It could just as well have been champagne I raised to the New Year, impatient to see what it would bring.

The college

It was quite eerie wandering round the unfinished, empty college with Mike. Beautifully planned and soundly built, the flagship of European Union Aid, it had offices for each department, student accommodation, teaching rooms, admin offices and a kitchen and dining block as well as staff housing.

"When will they come back?" I enquired anxiously eyeing the empty offices and bungalows – as though they never might.

"The students?"

"Staff, students – anybody."

"The Swazis usually rush home to plough as soon as the rains arrive," began Mike brightly, more at ease with this kind of exchange and happy to share his local knowledge, "This year of course, they can't, so I don't know what they're going to do."

"Wasn't there any rain?"

"Plenty, that's the whole irony of the situation. But when the old king died in August, everyone was forbidden to plough. It's part of Swazi tradition; when the king dies, the men are expected shave their heads as a mark of respect, women too, and no one must disturb the period of mourning by working."

"Oh, I thought there seemed to be an awful lot of bald people around. You can't mean the entire country has been at a standstill since last August? Surely if they don't plough, there'll be nothing to eat?"

"More than likely but here tradition outweighs even hunger."

"That's crazy!"

"You'll learn soon enough. It stretches into every aspect of their lives, this tradition business. Unfortunately, they also want the trappings of twentieth century Western life and the two aren't always compatible."

"Does that happen every time a king dies?"

"The last time that happened, before this one, I mean, was over eighty years ago. That's when this one's father died and King Sobhuza inherited so I don't suppose anyone even remembers what they did then. Swazi law and custom has never been written down so I should think whoever is in charge can more or less make it up as he goes along. There's no one left alive to contradict him."

"But what about industry and administration and so on. Everything seemed to be working OK in Mbabane."

"That's different. But the land, Swazi Nation Land, that more or less means the king. People can only work it if the chiefs allocate it to them, so if the chiefs want to show how loyal they are…"

17

"That is really feudal!"

"Now you're getting the idea but in the meantime, how about some twentieth century shopping down the supermarket?"

"The town boasts a supermarket? Thank goodness for that."

"I wouldn't call it a town. More of a village really. Come to think of it, perhaps I wouldn't even call Skonkwane's a supermarket but it's all we've got at the moment. Come on, I'll drive you down."

We drove the three kilometres to Nhlangano down a rutted, dusty but beautiful red murrain road with Jacaranda in full blossom.. When we got there, it took about three minutes to drive through the actual town from one end to the other, passing a Post Office, the supermarket, a bank, a filling station and a sprinkling of frontier type shops selling everything from window frames and axes to butter and brassieres. I felt as though we'd wandered onto the set of some Hollywood B movie, a make-believe cowboy frontier town with only facades fronting the street. If I looked behind them, I might find nothing there. The throng of pedestrians though, dispelled any fantasy of Hollywood or any other Western town. The place was teeming with "month end" shoppers of all shades from light brown to an almost purple blackness with a sprinkling of red-faced whites in khaki shorts and knee socks. Many of the older Swazi women wore the voluminous black pleated skirts, bright red patterned upper cloths and beehive hairdos, which marked them out as married matrons. Some men standing at the bus stop were wearing sarong-like skirts, split to the thigh, bare breasted bar their bead neck-bands and brightly coloured woollen ribbons worn diagonally across their chests tied with shoulder knots of gaudy pom-poms. Some had upright feathers in their hair while others carried very business like briefcases and umbrellas; a handsome people, small boned and very erect, secure in their own identity.

On an open space, a small but colourful African market added a further touch of colour with the usual

19

mixture of freshly harvested fruit and vegetables, old clothes and cooking stoves next to medicine men selling lurid powders, roots and skins and unrecognisable, mummified leathery creatures hanging down on ropes like cave bats. Then came the food stalls selling roast yams or gourds of thick sour milk. A little way out of town, at the end of a small golf course, stood the Hotel Casino, a modest complex rather self consciously cocooned in its splendid grounds. They both seemed entirely out of place, somehow.

"It's to capture the South African market." Mike said, reading my thoughts. "Like I said, gambling isn't allowed in the Republic so they come over the border which makes it a good money-spinner for Swaziland, an important part of the national income, in fact. This one isn't a patch on the ones up north in the Ezilwini Valley, of course, but it helps the local economy."

I opted to find my own way home. I wanted to explore the shops and the town, to savour new experiences and to do it at my own pace. Anyway, it was easy enough to find the way back. There was only one road.

I was almost home when I saw a lot of people gathered on the hillside opposite the college. It looked like a funeral though it was too far away to see clearly. A crowd of people were gathered in a cattle pen and a long wooden box was being carried towards it by men in black suits. My curiosity gave me the courage to ask a young Swazi passer-by if it was indeed a funeral.

"No, Mama," he laughed, "It's a wedding! Come and join us. I am also going there. You are welcome."

I had my doubts about that. Strangers couldn't just barge in, I protested. It wasn't barging, it was a sharing of joy he assured me. This was Swaziland and celebrations welcomed everyone.

"How very kind of you. I'd love to come."

It seemed the Swazis really did keep open house for celebrations, if you could call a field with a cattle kraal "open house". They were delighted that I was interested. A child was sent running for a chair from one of the homesteads and a great fuss made placing it where I could see what was happening in the kraal. And there I sat in solitary splendour, the only one honoured with a chair. The feeling of splendour was not to last. The field had a very steep slope and the kitchen chair a particularly slippery plastic seat. It was hard to concentrate on what was happening in the kraal and at the same time judge when the chair and I were about to part company. I didn't want to risk hurting their feelings by abandoning it altogether but every time I half rose to readjust my position, it was taken as particular enthusiasm on my part to get a better view of the proceedings and any onlookers who dared to stand in front, were sharply pushed out of the way.

Still, it did undoubtedly give me a good vantage point of what my newly acquired guide termed the sacred centre of Swazi life. Traditionally, he said, the kraal was where the grain was stored underground, where their precious cattle were kept safe and ancestors buried. The actual Christian wedding had taken place the day before and this was the Swazi follow on. Women, normally, weren't allowed to set foot in the kraal, he said, but today they were included while some of the wedding formalities took place.

As long as they didn't presume too much, I thought, as I saw them sitting on the ground among the cow pats and flies with only straw mats between them and the mud and positioned well below the level of the men on the benches. The women all wore national dress of sorts; scrawny chested old men wore their sarongs and pom-poms while others, the younger ones on the whole, were dressed in full Western suits with waistcoats and ties. It was a mixture of traditional and western. The long wooden box I'd taken for the dear departed had pride of place in the middle. To my relief, it didn't contain a corpse. In a reversal of Western custom, it was full of presents the bride had to give to her numerous new in-laws, the whole extended family according to their rank. Some got a blanket, some enamel bowls and mugs, some woven mats down to the lowest ranks who only got grass besoms.

The bride herself was the only woman not in national dress. She wore a beautiful white wedding gown which was trailing in the muddy hoof marks of the kraal and needed retrieving from the cowpats now and then. Not surprisingly, it was beginning to look somewhat bedraggled as were her white satin shoes. At the end of the presentations and long speeches, she walked round the enclosure with her head so deeply bowed, I thought she must have dropped something, the wedding ring perhaps? Could I help to find it, I offered? This suggestion was greeted with delighted laughter. She was bowed, the young man explained, because she must always be humble before her in-laws. In any case, looking another person straight in the eye was very rude, a sign of great disrespect. That shook me. What of Western theories about eye contact and honesty or evasion, I wondered? How were those going to fit in? And what else was going to stand my precious beliefs on their head?

The Club

In the days of Empire, every little territory, no matter how far from "civilization", had its club for its overseas civil servants and Nhlangano was no exception. Although the Empire has long gone and most expatriate civil servants with it, many of the clubs still remain. Often run down and faded, shadows of their former selves but now open to the whole community and still serving as a meeting place to form friendships, exchange local gossip, have a drink, play darts or tennis, form a cricket team or enjoy a leisurely, home cooked Sunday lunch.

Mike disapproved of clubs. He said they were bastions of imperialism, the last outposts of the Raj which was probably true. I got the impression that he would have liked me to adopt similar principles but, Raj or no Raj, I needed a social life outside the confines of the college. There was nothing else on offer locally; no cinema, no library or TV, no alternative activities of any kind so on the following afternoon I made my own way down there.

The clubhouse had seen better days. It was a rather run down single story building with a clay tennis court and a small swimming pool next to the Casino's modest golf course. Chickens were scratching for grubs in the driveway and on the cricket pitch while a group of Swazi children played in the caretaker's compound. No one else seemed to be around but the door stood wide open.

The inside was as shabby as the outside with a large, almost empty room leading into a bar and a games room. The clink of billiard balls kissing was the only sound to be heard. I followed the direction and found a lone European player practicing. Evenings and weekends were the times the club came into its own, he said. He was only there because it was his day off from working on the new road through the valley that McAlpines was building and he didn't know what to do with himself. He went behind the bar, poured us both a drink, signed a list and chatted. He assured me the club was multiracial, now open to any member of the community although one still had to be sponsored! It was oversubscribed with Europeans like him at present because of the road building. He suggested I come back at the weekend to meet some of the regulars so that's exactly what I did and found myself overwhelmed with questions and invitations to just about everything. In such a small community newcomers, though welcome, were always sniffed around to get their dimensions, their political odour, their potential place in the hierarchy of the established social order – among the whites, of course. My inability to connect any sort of ball to racquet, club or bat clearly ruled me out of the sporting fraternity. As a full time working woman I was ruled out of the ladies bridge and coffee mornings but I was quite happy just to use the club to get to know people and have the occasional drink. I did though, eventually join the bowling group and enjoyed it hugely.

 The Kirks promptly took me under their generous wing, especially Margaret who was the voice of authority in the family. Having occupied the large bungalow immediately next to the club for the past fifteen years, with Rob being an ODA technical teacher at the local secondary school, they had their pulse on everything that went on in the village, among the whites, anyway. Almost the first thing they did was to invite me to their son's eleventh birthday party.

Margaret loved both her children passionately, devouring them with her ambitious plans for their future, directing their friendships and their social life. To this end, unlike David, they were not sent to Waterford, the highly regarded International School in Mbabane,but went instead to the most prestigious white boarding school in South Africa, care of ODA. Now they were home on holiday, the birthday had given her an opportunity for another display of motherly pride.

"It's just a wee celebration, nothing special." Margaret assured me when I hesitated about the intrusion. "Just come to the house."

On Sunday, when I got to there with my small present nicely wrapped, wearing my patent leather pumps and my one posh dress ready for the party, I found a scene of feverish activity. For a brief moment I thought I'd arrived just in time to help them unexpectedly move house. In the road outside various other adult European guests, a small assortment of children and servants were all scurrying round loading things onto a couple of lorries. Everyone wore serviceable shorts or slacks. Apparently the party was in the form of a picnic some miles away beside some farmer's dam. Someone might have made it clear, I thought crossly, feeling totally out of place. Without thinking, I was still reacting in European fashion to the word 'party' so consequently, I could do nothing but watch.

There seemed to be more paraphernalia than I had in my entire bungalow. Some oil drums, which had been sliced in half horizontally with legs soldered on, did service for the braais. Servants heaved sacks of charcoal and wood, folding tables and chairs, bins of ice, crates of drink, boxes, boxes and more boxes and loaded them. Margaret was getting increasingly exasperated with the two servants.

"Take care of those glasses, Philomen. They're not plastic you know. And what did you do with the meat master gave you? Is it loaded?"

Philomen looked at the piled bakkie and shrugged his

shoulders.

"Och, never mind then. Alistair, have you got all the things you want darling? Bikes, cricket things, fishing rods, your presents? We don't want to have to come back for anything, you know."

The eleven-year old birthday boy carried out a large plastic bin overflowing with his birthday parcels. The other guests took care of the smaller items like cool-bags of food, toys, extra anonymous boxes and finally two boats. Dogs and children ran about getting in everyone's way. When both lorries were loaded to everyone's satisfaction, which meant in reality that they could take no more, they took off for the dam while the rest followed in various cars.

In a short while, we turned into a rough farm track and made for the water shining the other side of a small copse. Since the servants had been left behind, the unloading took even longer than the loading. Grave decisions had to be taken about the positioning of the tables between the trees and the placement of the bins of ice. Side tables were erected for standing oil and multitudes of sauces, spices and condiments. Bottles of mineral water also stood at the ready for throwing on the hot embers for that explosive burst of smoke which gave that authentic smoky flavour to the meat much favoured by aficionados of southern braais.

The oldest members of the party were settled comfortably in armchairs, the youngest sent to the dam with their boats and lifejackets. It was mainly a gathering of adults and an opportunity to pay tribute to Margaret's motherhood and to her skill as hostess. Out came the boxes. Out came the damask tablecloths with matching serviettes; out came the crystal glasses, the porcelain and the silver cutlery and the bottle of champagne in its own silver ice bucket. Glyndebourne transposed to the African bush came to mind.

Each new item unpacked was granted due admiration while Margaret glowed with pleasure. Salads were given a last minute dressing, fruit polished and glace cherries artistically arranged on trifles and iced cakes. The birthday cake had obviously had a bad journey judging by Margaret's hysterics and needed some emergency surgery. There was a united sigh of relief when all the preparations were finally complete and the guests could get down to some serious drinking till the charcoal had reached the critical level of embers for the steaks and boerewurst.

As I helped to set the places, I felt as though I was taking part in a Russian play, half expecting someone to start a bored conversation about the fate of a birch grove or a cherry orchard and the state of the peasantry. Actually, I wasn't far off the mark.

"Mustn't forget the plastic covers," Margaret

29

remarked, covering up the food, "You know what the flies are like around here – and those people."

"What people?"

Everyone seemed to know what she meant except me.

"Those Africans from the homesteads of course. Look, they've turned up already."

Bright little brown eyes under curly mops were peeping through the bushes and quickly disappeared again when they caught your eye. Free entertainment and the smell of meat cooking had brought the Swazi children running.

"Get yourselves out of here, you cheeky bairns," shouted Margaret and the children disappeared and then bobbed up somewhere else. More shouting followed before finally, to my horror, the dogs were sent to chase them and they rushed off screaming in terror.

Over the gins and beers, the talk turned immediately to the shortcomings of the locals as it often did when none were present. This was interspersed with dogs' barking, taped music and laughter from the children playing by the dam. It was my first real introduction to Us and Them. And where did I belong? In neither camp, I hoped. And with that thought, I had, for now to be satisfied.

No one noticed when I wandered off among the trees

enjoying the clean smell of the eucalyptus even though I'd been told they were pests with a mighty thirst. A new plantation, they said, could lower the water table considerably and at least one farmer they knew had to have a weekly water tanker brought to his house because of that. Even so, to me every forested hill was beautiful, eucalyptus or pine, particularly in the mornings when the sunrise sent long parallel shadows through the pine forests till the spiky black silhouettes turned silver-green.

At the edge of the dam, the children were still playing. The boats and bikes had quickly lost their appeal and lay abandoned. The birthday presents lay scattered on the shore among a litter of torn wrapping paper.

"Oh, hi," said Alistair cheerfully. "Thanks for your birthday present."

"You're welcome, Alistair. Do you like it?"

"I did, only it's at the bottom of the dam now and we can't fish it out." and he turned back to his water battle.

Never mind, I wanted to say. It was only a small thing, a novelty I picked up at Heathrow. But no one was listening.

New beginnings

When David arrived from Nairobi, he settled into his school, Waterford Khamlaba, one of the famous United World Colleges; situated at the top of a hill in Mbabane. Founded in the 60's in opposition to the apartheid education practiced in the Republic, it had an international, multi cultural mixture of students and particularly, a community service programme which I liked. As part of the curriculum, each student had to take part in some community project or other. This could be something simple such as helping people to read the charts at an eye clinic, heavier stuff like lending a hand to build new classrooms or clinics or perhaps some adult literacy sessions. There was plenty of choice and plenty needed. For his part, David and a few of the other students opted to take some disabled, orphan children on a regular basis and teach them to swim at the Cuddle Puddle, the hot spring pool of one of the Ezulwini Valley hotels. To begin with, seeing the teenagers just diving in, the little ones followed without waiting for swimming aids and sank, of course, in a trail of bubbles. I wonder if they thought being rescued coughing and spluttering was an essential part of the lesson. Not that they minded.

This particular group of children, some with encephalitis, some with polio, were ones who had been abandoned at the hospital. Unfortunately, according to the paediatrician I met, that happened all too often. Many families believed disabled children were the result of a curse and they hid them away. Sometimes mothers took them to the hospital for some treatment or other, many using a false name and just abandoned them like a piece of left luggage. Without any other suitable facilities at that time, a few had been there more than two years. In a country without a written record of all its citizens, parliamentary voting by head counting and postal boxes for addresses it wasn't easy or even possible at that time to trace the parents if they didn't want to be found. In 1989 the first SOS children's village was built in Swaziland by the Austrian charity founded to help children left orphaned by the second world war. It was built just below Waterford school in Mbabane to try to save abandoned children like these and of course, many more.

It was much the same story, Doctor McGrath told me, for trying to control sexual diseases. Tell a woman with some venereal disease that she should bring her partner for treatment for his "bad blood" and the chances were you never saw either of them again. And that was before the great scourge of HIV and AIDS from the 90s onwards left such a huge percentage of orphans in Swaziland they could no longer be ignored; Swaziland had the dubious honour of having sub Saharan Africa's highest rate of

HIV/AIDS.

Every other weekend was free for the Waterford students which meant I needed my car to fetch David home. After my unfortunate experience with cars in Kenya, I had decided to bring my little yellow Golf out as part of my shipping allowance, the major part, in fact. Now it needed to be fetched from the docks at Durban. I got a lift from the ever helpful Kirks, who were off for a weekend to visit their children and I eventually managed to claim my car. The authorities must have thought anyone crazy enough to ship a second hand car out from the UK to somewhere like South Africa, must be trying to import something illegal, possibly drugs. They had unscrewed every surface in the interior in their search and not put things back together very well. Still, it went and, after piles of paperwork and arguments about duty payable, I set off on the 250 miles or so back to Swaziland. It was my first experience of driving in South Africa and I was agreeably surprised about the state of the roads. If, as I was told, the Republic had concentrated on its infrastructure in order to deploy its troops to hot spots as quickly as possible, they had made a good job of it. What also surprised me, or perhaps shocked would be a more appropriate word, was the way almost all the houses had bars on their windows and were surrounded with high walls topped with razor wire as though expecting an attack of some sort.

The first 180 miles or so went very smoothly and after more than three hours of driving I decided to pull over in Dundee for a short rest. Since it was just by a bottle store, I thought I'd buy the Kirks some really nice wine or whiskey perhaps, as thanks for their help. The counter was manned by a large white Afrikaner youth who seemed not to speak English, ignored my request and gestured towards the door. Undaunted by this language problem, I pointed at the bottle I wanted but he just shook his head. The only customers in the shop were some Coloureds (hateful word) who explained to me, in good English, that he was only allowed to serve non whites. Whites were served in the shop next door – by a black man.

"Don't be so ridiculous! Just sell me that bottle of wine." I said.

"That's right lady! You tell him." the others joined in but still I left without the wine and I didn't call in next door.

Disaster struck a few miles up the road at Vryheid when the Golf decided it had had enough and simply came to a halt. It had the decency to stop in the town near what looked like a hotel so I decided to call it a day, get something to eat and a room for the night. It seemed a simple thing to do but when I walked into the hotel bar in search of the proprietor, about fifteen white male heads turned and stared at me in astonishment. This bar was not for ladies; they had to go to the room next door. So, in the face of this further lunatic discrimination, there I went and sat in splendid isolation waiting for the sandwich they had (reluctantly) agreed to make for me. A row of bottles was arranged behind the bar and since I wouldn't be driving any more that night, I chose an interesting looking gin. It was not available the barman told me, none of them were. The bottles were all empty, not due to sanctions, but because they were not allowed to display filled bottles in the ladies bar. Here the real alcohol was kept under the counter. The reason for this? The barman couldn't say except that it was the law.

Everyone was more than helpful the following morning, finding a mechanic and sending me on my way. I breathed a sigh of relief as I crossed the Swazi border as I always did thereafter. It felt so much more relaxed and comfortable. It was good to be back.

Now that I had wheels, I fell into the routine of fetching David from school on alternate week-ends when he was free, a total of eight hours driving per week-end. Luckily, he enjoyed his school and the time at home was mainly taken up with sport at the club. At least, that was the routine until the brand new valley road got so badly damaged and dangerous as the result of cyclone Demoina, I sometimes opted to cross the border and drive up through South Africa to the Oshoek border post to get to Mbabane which was a bit of a nightmare.

My Sinhalese ex husband's name of Salgado, which I had kept after my divorce, was Portugese in origin and it aroused deep suspicion in the South African border guards at the Mahamba crossing. Neighbouring Mozambique had been a Portuguese colony until 1975 so, with a name like that, I could well be up to no good and denied entry. Despite the availability of computers, there were always long delays while they went into a back room and looked me up on their lists of suspicious travellers and searched the car. On one occasion they confiscated a book I had with me saying it was on the list of prohibited literature. It was a harmless novel I was in the middle of reading, not some fiery political tract, but orders were orders they said. Unbelievably the children's book "Black Beauty" was also on the prohibited list! It must have been a world first for a fictional horse to be considered subversive or did they imagine the "Black Beauty" of the title was some kind of African Mata Hari? Extraordinary.

The other thing that eventually puzzled me was the small slit at the top of the envelopes of all my letters when they got to me. Someone suggested that that was where a probe was inserted to scrutinize the

38

contents though how letters addressed to Swaziland passed through South African security hands I had no idea. Or at least, not then. And all because I had an unwelcome name. Compared to the trauma of apartheid next door, the gunning down of schoolchildren, pass laws, forced removals and all the other brutalities, my little inconveniences were just a flea bite, hardly worth mentioning and my life was very happy.

I finally got to meet all my Swazi colleagues the majority of whom were educated, confident and welcoming women. In a country even more chauvinist than Kenya, my previous experience, Swazi women really had a raw deal. They had the status of children, couldn't own property in their own right, couldn't have a passport or bank account without their husband's or father's permission, could face punishment from the chiefs or get thrown off a bus just for wearing trousers and it was legal for a husband to beat his wife. But worst of all, by Swazi Law and Custom, was the lack of rights of Swazi women over the fate of their children. Even those born outside marriage could become the property of the father if he wanted, once the right lobola price had been negotiated and paid to the mother's father, the traditional guardian of those children. Sometimes this encouraged the biological father to wait till they were older to claim his rights over his children, especially a daughter nearing marriageable age so he could claim the lobola that would be paid for her. Being forced into an underage marriage, even as young as 14, by the biological father, usually to a financially secure older man, is permitted under Swazi Law and Custom (which usually overrules civil law where it is not). This is just what happened to the sister of one of the lecturers, I was told, her daughter now spirited away to the home of the father's mother.

Sad though that was, it was a rarity on the campus. The children born out of wedlock were being brought up by mothers whose choice was not to marry or even, in one extreme case, to acknowledge who had fathered her children so she had charge of their upbringing. Laws were different for those who were married by Roman Dutch law as most of my Christian colleagues were but the social pressures of Swazi Law and Custom still seemed to predominate. Family arrangements were also different. Several of my married colleagues had their children with them while the husbands lived and worked elsewhere. The reverse could be true when the children were at good schools up north living with their extended family and their lecturer mother visiting at weekends. I only ever remember some of my male colleagues having complete families living on campus and they were very much in the minority.

Women, the smart ones anyway, employed a number of tricks to get round the male dominated system. When I sold my car to a colleague, she said I had to pretend I'd sold it to a sympathetic male cousin of hers so her estranged husband couldn't lay claim to it. Something similar happened to one of the nuns in the RE department. On her study year in the US she had saved enough to buy a precious car when she got back only to have the local priest lay claim to it. The dilemma was resolved when she left the church and kept the car! On the whole though, the college was an island of calm, protected from the harshest applications of male chauvinism which were more to be found in the rural countryside than the towns or perhaps I just didn't notice till it came knocking on my door.

In keeping with the split personality of the whole country, the dual laws, Roman Dutch and Swazi, the two kinds of marriage Civil and traditional, the two kinds of dress, Western and Swazi, the college tried to embrace much of the national culture as well as introducing the students to western ideas. The Home Economics department under the fierce rule of Mrs Msibi for instance, used everything from electric cookers to clay pots on three stones, modern kitchens to clay and wattle rondavels, western hygiene to traditional remedies. Arts and Crafts included weaving straw mats as well as more conventional work. Agriculture, Science, Maths, Languages, Domestic Science,(which the male students also had to do) Music, History, Geography, Child Development and Education were all catered for and the students had to take them all. It was a heavy load.

It was a heavy load for the lecturers too without the usual teaching aids which were still en route from Europe somewhere. Those were pre computer, printers, mobile phones and credit cards days but, at least, in this brand new college I had expected there to be some duplicating facilities, white boards instead of chalk, and Overhead Projectors to cut down on endless repetition and lack of visual aids. Not yet. On their way.

Despite this total state of unreadiness, one day we were abruptly told we were to be visited by the Prince of Luxemburg. I have no idea how all that came about but it caused an unexpected flurry of activity. All the college desks suddenly came out of storage, floors were swept, gardens weeded, windows cleaned. At the last moment someone remembered the portraits of the late king Sobhuza and the Prime Minister were not displayed so three inch nails were obtained and an attempt was made to hammer them into the wall. In vain. I remembered I had a couple of stick on hooks left over and rushed home to fetch them as the advance party was seen drawing up at the college gates. We quickly stuck them and the portraits on the wall whereupon the visiting Minister of Protocol, a pompous, weedy man in a pinstriped brown suit pointed out that the portraits were on the same level whereas the PM should be below that of the king. This posed a bit of a problem since the hooks couldn't come out without taking bits of the wall with them. It was resolved by removing the screws and wire on the back of one picture, repositioning them and hanging the PM the regulation three inches lower than the king. Not satisfied with that, the Protocol Minister then wanted to know why we had given the PM a more ornate frame than the king. Looking totally bemused, everyone kept silent. By this time I had had enough and said tartly, "Because he's alive and the king is dead." That took care of that.

Determined to keep himself in a job, he then ordered everyone to line up outside according to rank, men and women separately. Much to my surprise, everyone seemed to know exactly who ranked above or below them. I can't remember where that placed me but it was probably below the lowest ranks. The harder the poor Prince of Luxemburg tried to keep things friendly and informal, the harder the brown pinstripe man worked to keep formality alive and well and working in Swaziland. He had come as a representative of the EU to see how the college was progressing but wasn't allowed to speak to any of the staff lined up. At least no long speeches were made, just a short announcement that they were going to tour the college and we were therefore dismissed and could get back to where we belonged.

After about four or five months, much to my delight, the college was joined by another ODA expatriate couple, Michael and Joy Oldridge. Mike came to teach Maths. Apart from Science, the college then had their full complement of ODA personnel but it was still not finished or fully equipped. Official EEC sanctions prevented anything being bought from neighbouring South Africa. It had to be ordered and shipped all the way from Europe and so was subject to long delays. This was anathema to the impatient Swazi who loved to celebrate and finished or not, they were going to party and show off their beautiful college

The opening of the college

We met before dawn, the black bull and I. He was being led submissively into the kitchen yard; a huge beast with a glossy blue-black hide, steam rising from his flanks and the smell of the farmyard about him. Or was it the smell of fear as they led him to his death? How was it, I wondered, that compared to most other parts of the world, the bulls of Africa were so docile? Of course they had to be to wander the countryside as they did herded by small children they could have killed so easily with a slight toss of their horns. And this bull? His misfortune was that he was black and black bulls were considered auspicious. Each year at the Incwala ceremony, I'd heard, the soldiers of the king were supposed to wrestle one to the ground to kill him as proof of their strength and virility, mirroring the strength of the nation. But more of that later. How was this one to be killed? They were certainly not going to wrestle him to the ground Incwala fashion. Neither did the college boast a stun gun or any sort of gun for that matter. Were they going to cut his throat and let him bleed to death slowly and painfully before their eyes? That could take a long time and he needed to be roast, chopped up and served at table before twelve. It was hard enough to picture the poor undersized kitchen helpers who normally did nothing more strenuous than dipping dirty dishes into the sink,

45

having the energy to wring the neck of a chicken let alone dealing with a bull. It was all very mysterious but doubtless they would find a way of dealing with the problem just as I had found a way to deal with mine.

It was all on account of the official opening of the college some nine months after my arrival. Although it wasn't entirely finished or fully equipped yet, especially with modern catering machinery for the kitchens, which was still being shipped from Europe due to sanctions against apartheid, Vilakazi the Principal had made up his mind that the college needed to be opened right now with due pomp and ceremony. So, in true Swazi fashion, as the Chief, his word had to be obeyed and the deed was to be performed on 30th of September by Prince Bhekimpi Dlamini, the new Prime Minister. For all the women lecturers – and that included me, this meant that we were expected to forget education for the next few weeks and revert to our true role in Swazi life, working in the kitchen preparing mountains of food for all the guests.

Vilakasi summoned all the lecturers together and announced that the male lecturers would be responsible for the furniture, the ushering and the drinks; the Art department for all the decorations and tableware and the women lecturers with all the catering for the great event. I could, perhaps, have opted out but it was an ideal opportunity to show sisterly solidarity so I smiled and wondered what he had in mind for me to do.

Since Vilakasi didn't really trust my culinary skill with important things like cooking meat or even making the jelly and custard, which I later came to realise were a vital part of any Swazi celebration, (I blame the missionaries) the truly important things like roast chickens, stewed mutton, maize pap, scones, fairy cakes and buns were to be the province of the Home Economics department which boasted traditional wood stoves, a camp kitchen and modern electric cookers. The Art department would be responsible for the decorations and setting the tables while the infamous jellies and custards went to the Science Department for no good reason that I could see. I was beginning to hope everything had been covered without my involvement. It was not to be. The Education Department, all two of us, were allocated the making of the salad, by which was meant coleslaw. That was to be our particular task. Details to be worked out at the next meeting.

But the next meeting seemed to be a long time coming and Home Economics in particular were getting anxious about the quantities of provisions required. How many were they to cater for? Try as we might, we couldn't get the Principal to give us a straight answer. A true Swazi traditionalist, he would shrug his shoulders and sweep his arms expansively muttering about local custom, Government Ministers, members of the royal family, but never an actual or even approximate number. Since a sizeable percentage of the million or so population of Swaziland was royal, the late king having had more than sixty wives and more offspring than anyone probably cared to count, not to mention the uncles, aunts, second cousins and the rest of the kin, the catering committee's collective hearts began to sink.

As the great day drew ever nearer, panic began to set in surrounded as we were with feverish activity. The Sibhaca dancers banged away on their drums and the choir sang morning and afternoon. All the stoves were ready, wood collected, tin baths scrubbed, new dustbins bought, chickens given the last rites but still no answers. A showdown was demanded. What provisions had to be purchased? How many scones would have to be baked? How many guests were expected? Almost at the point of female mutiny – unheard of in chauvinist Swaziland – Vilakazi did finally come up with a number. He had perfected that old teaching trick of speaking sufficiently softly for his students to have to pay close attention to what he was saying. Questioned directly, he gave a figure, which I didn't quite catch – or thought I didn't.

"What did he say?" I asked the person sitting next to me.

"Two thousand."

Two thousand? I must have missed something. Scones perhaps?

"Two thousand what?" I said, totally confused.

"People, of course," said my neighbour impatiently, anxious to catch what else Vilakasi was saying in his quiet manner.

"Two … two … two thousand? You want me to make coleslaw for two thousand people?" I burst out, flabbergasted, "What with?"

Vilakazi paused in mid sentence and gave me a pitying look, confirmed in his opinion of me as a culinary liability.

"Cabbages and carrots?" he suggested tentatively looking for confirmation to members of the Home Economics department.

"No, I mean how do I make it … what with?" Now Vilakazi was in unchartered territory. He hesitated,

"I believe the kitchen has a couple of cheese graters or whatever you call those things … Anyway," he went on more brightly, "There are plenty of students to help you."

I had nightmare visions of a line of students all waiting to take their turn with two cheese graters to make coleslaw, God help us, for two … I couldn't get my head round it … for two thousand!

I passed the rest of the meeting in stunned silence trying to picture the mountain of coleslaw that needed to be produced – and all from the basic ingredients. Jane Motsa, my colleague, was appointed to help me and offered to organise a group of students. She had been paying close attention to Vilakasi and reported that cabbages, carrots and students would be delivered the day after tomorrow. Some of my female colleagues were already planning to work from three or four in the morning, some all night for several nights making samp and scones and cakes. I had no idea where to start.

I went home and made myself a strong cup of coffee. That did nothing for me. Then I had a large brandy and then another and somehow the problem didn't seem so bad any more. Anyway, I was determined that I wasn't going to be beaten. It wasn't only the Africans who didn't like to lose face. I was going to work this out – if only I could think how.

Really, nothing short of electric kitchen machinery could solve this one and that was still en route from Europe on the high seas somewhere. Where on earth would one find something like that in this little backwater of Africa? Who needed to cater for large numbers? Why, the Casino, of course – for the gamblers! But would they agree to help us? I could ask that nice man, Robin, I'd met at the club. Wasn't he something to do with the Casino? They must have shredding machinery at the hotel … surely … and if I put it to them that this was an opportunity to show the local community how public spirited they were, helping out for the honour of the town … They could only say no. But Robin must have been persuasive because they didn't.

And the following day Jane, my colleague, six students, eight huge sacks of cabbages, four sacks of carrots, six brand new, shiny, galvanized dustbins and umpteen plastic bowls and I arrived at the casino. They suddenly realised what they'd let themselves in for and blanched somewhat at the sight of us but stuck to their agreement. To keep us out of the way of the work of the kitchen, they put the equipment and machines out in the yard, connected a hose pipe and we all set to work: washing, cutting, shredding, packing, washing, cutting, shredding, packing. It took us the best part of eight hours, all through the worst of the heat with no protection from the sun, all working solidly, students and staff – but we did it. The Casino kitchen workers were most impressed. We looked at the results of our labours and all agreed that barring a miracle along the lines of the loaves and the fishes, even the six dustbins full would never stretch to even five hundred guests let alone two thousand! But we had stuck to our allotted task and finished off every cabbage leaf. All it needed now was to mix it with mayonnaise the following morning. And that's when I came upon the doomed black bull in the kitchen yard before dawn and having met him face to face, I decided I couldn't bring myself to eat him, celebrations or no celebrations.

My next allotted task was to wait on the big wigs invited including the Prime Minister. All the tables were full of food: mountains of roast chicken and mutton, chunks of the famous bull at the top table together with its black tripe, a special delicacy, salad, scones, semp, jellies and – since alcohol was off limits – hundreds and hundreds of bottles of pop but no one had thought of bottle openers, teeth being the usual implement which seemed somewhat inappropriate in present circumstances. The kitchen staff pleaded ignorance, so I had to run home and fetch mine and spent the rest of the celebrations trying to cope with everyone's impatient demands to get at their drink, including the PM. It was the only time I ever got near the hand of power and what power! I wasn't aware at the time that Prince Bhekimpi had just become the new PM after helping to engineer a palace coup deposing the Queen Regent, Dzeliwe, known as Ndlovukazi (the Great She-Elephant) to the nation. This was destined to have a personal involvement for me later but for the present I was totally occupied with fizzy pop.

Somehow, when the feasting was over and the mess

cleared away, I expected some congratulations on our amazing triumph, some sign of gratitude for all the huge efforts and at least, a polite note of thanks sent to the Casino. None materialized. Instead, I had the feeling that somehow, Vilakasi disapproved. It was hard to put my finger on it but I was sensitive to a certain coolness. With the best will in the world, in the time available, we would never have coped without modern machinery, the same kind of machinery due to arrive shortly in the college kitchen. Would it have tasted any better chopped by hand flavoured perhaps with the blood of a few grated fingers? Or perhaps it was because this woman had used her initiative and, in Vilakasi's chauvinist world, that was not supposed to happen. Or because he thought that just because I was white, I had used that fact to gain privileges the others couldn't? Knowing the calibre of my colleagues, I didn't believe that and anyway, if it helped the college did it matter how? Wasn't that what I was there for?

The demolition of the black bull.

The hazards of teaching

Whenever teaching practice supervision came around, as happened twice a year, my thoughts invariably turned to toilets. This was due to bitter, or should I say painful, experience? I quote from the diary I kept when I first arrived in Swaziland but sadly, failed to keep up:

Thursday, February 3rd, 1983.

"In a state of shock.

Today, after only three weeks in College, I was sent out to my first primary school in rural Swaziland and find it hard to believe what I saw. The classroom was bare of furniture except for three dilapidated tables and one bench. Most of the 60 or so children in the class were perched on piles of pieces of broken breeze-blocks precariously balanced. There were generally about three jagged pieces of block on top of each other and sometimes, when the children sprang to attention to answer a question or stretched over to do something, the piles fell over almost injuring the child next to them if they didn't quickly jump out of the way.

There were no displays on the walls and no equipment apart from bottle tops for counting and some match boxes. The parents are supposed to supply the books but few can afford to. Nor can they afford the R100 p.a. for equipment and furniture for the school. But the children were so eager and all beautifully dressed in their spotless uniforms, my heart went out to them. I don't know how any child can learn anything under these conditions but somehow, they do.

Without equipment, teaching was chalk and talk and chorusing but at least those weren't a danger to life and limb. There was no toilet block either or if there was I didn't see it or more to the point, smell it. I saw the children go into the bushes to defecate and I presumed I was expected to do the same."

It was certainly not a situation that would be helped by any fatuous advice on my part about different teaching methods, that's for sure. I should, perhaps, have suggested abandoning the lethal classroom and taking a lesson outside but that wasn't what first came to mind. Digging a few long drop loos to remedy the lack of basic sanitation, the cause of so much childhood disease, would have improved the health and the educational standards of the children without any doubt, but that was beyond the remit of the poor teacher and of me.

A relic of the distant past? Unfortunately not. More than 30 years later, in 2016, Swazi Schools Project, a charity, is telling its donors, "our next priorities are to build toilets for the staff at Luhhumaneni (school) and two new classrooms…" I doubt they're keeping their legs crossed in the meantime.

Not all the schools were like that first one. In fact, it was the only one I came across; a baptism of fire, I suspect. "Let's see what she makes of that one.". Some had water laid on, decent sanitation and even electricity though there was always the problem of paying for these facilities once the Overseas Aid that had installed them was finished and the workers gone home.

Our model primary school.

Up on the hillside not that far from Nhlangano were the ribs of disused dams embracing waterless hollows; bones of sluice gates marking the grave of yet another European Project that collapsed soon after the Aid workers left. A leather factory stood mouldering. The hard working initiators probably returned to the West feeling good about themselves because they'd done their bit setting up this new project to uplift the poor of the developing world. The furniture workshop down the road is silent and deserted. Left to carry on independently, the tools were gradually filched until the whole enterprise collapsed. Ten people were thrown out of work but whoever stole them could no doubt set up on his own or sell the tools to get what most Swazi desired – a motor car.

I had always thought there was a concept of communalism among the clans but I was sadly disabused. Had the concept of personal greed also been imported from the west? Certainly unity and social pressure for the common good has lessened, especially since many of the chiefs and those in government or part of the royal power base could hardly be said to set an example. Rather, theirs was an unparalleled example of self-aggrandizement and greed.

The Canadians thought they'd learnt from other's mistakes and covered everything with their local rural water scheme; pre-project consultation and agreement, simple technology, maintenance training and plenty of spare parts for the follow up. The chiefs consulted with every household and school. Everyone recognized that clean water was essential, the terms of the scheme were agreed and there need be no more walking for miles to the river to fetch unsafe water. No sooner had the Canadians returned home than a couple of the local families refused to contribute to the cost of the diesel fuel to keep the pumps working (or perhaps they just didn't have the money) and the area Chief did nothing to resolve the problem. Naturally enough, the other families objected to shouldering the extra financial burden and in no time at all we were back to the cheaper option, to women and children doing what they had always done, fetching water from the river and pupils being taken out of classes to fill the school water tanks and those of the teachers' houses.

Would that be the fate of all my efforts to improve the way that the children of Swaziland were educated, I wondered? Back to the beatings and "repeat after me"? Don't ask questions and don't think for yourselves. I hoped not. At least I wanted to try to do something for the disabled children hidden away. But what? Special Education was one of my fields of experience and expertise and I felt strongly about it. Little did I know at that point how much the catastrophe of HIV/AIDS would exacerbate that situation in the decade to come and finally thrust it to the forefront where it could no longer be ignored.

The only disabled person I occasionally saw around the campus was a relative of someone on the staff. He propelled himself around in a wheelchair and

59

whenever the man with the withered legs passed by, some of the Swazi children would scream, run away, jeer or even throw stones. It didn't help that his speech resembled crude noises but that was the way it was, here in the more traditional, rural south of Swaziland. Disability was seen by many as the curse of the ancestors or the outcome of witchcraft. I found it all very distressing and wondered what, if anything, I could do. When I did try to intervene, it ended in something of a humiliation. I saw the disabled young man pulling himself along on hands and knees because his wheelchair had broken and needed repairing or replacing, hardly surprising given the rough state of the paths and roads. Ever ready to stick my nose in, and given that we had over three hundred students and it was close to Christmas, I thought as well as donating towards helping him myself, the students might also like to help the poor man. I couldn't suggest outright donations but perhaps they might be interested in buying some Christmas cards and helping that way? They all seemed enthusiastic so I set about making some with sketches of the college on the front and offered them cheaply, more as a token of help for the poor man than making a sizable dent in the cost of a replacement chair. Imagine my surprise when I was summoned to the Principal's office and told I must get back all the cards sold and return the money, no

60

explanation given even when asked for. What was it I failed to understand about the Swazi psyche? So I duly gave them back their money, told the students to keep the cards and the young man kept crawling around for a month or so and then disappeared.

Education was not compulsory and parents, at that time, were expected to pay right from grade 1 in the primary school to the end of Form V in the secondary if they ever got that far though in fact, only a lucky 25% ever did. True, the grade 1 fees were very modest but then one has to start counting such things as uniforms, books, stationery and the ubiquitous building fund, otherwise known as bribing the Head. That was one way of getting your child into school, but the more usual method was for the Head to see if the child came up to his or her waist and then ask them to lift their right arm over their head and touch their left ear. If they couldn't do that, they were considered not mature enough to start school and told to come back next year.

Since 80% of the Swazis in the Shiselweni district were subsistence farmers, it was small wonder that hard-pressed parents or grannies failed to press for an education for a handicapped child or, at best, left it for the Missions and churches to pick up the pieces. The point of the enormous financial sacrifice of the family is to educate someone to be in a position to help the rest of the family and keep you in your old age in the absence of a welfare state. Only the fittest are likely to succeed.

A glimmer of a chance to do something happened when Leonard Nkambule, my latest counterpart in the Education department became Deputy Principal. My post was advisory "leading from behind" as ODA put it, teaching my Swazi counterpart to take over. While in the Education Department, Leonard had been particularly eager to learn and use any skills I could pass on especially when it came to time -tabling, record keeping and creating new courses. Then just as I felt he was really comfortable in his role, he was kicked upstairs to be Deputy Principal. Of course I was pleased about his promotion though, once again, it left a gap in the department.

The college was not yet complete and the EEC officials actually asked for suggestions of what else the college would like added. I knew immediately what I would like included. I described the pre – school set up I was most familiar with at Sussex University which took children (part time) from the age of two and a half and formed part of the Education, Child Development and Psychology department .With its one way window where the children's behaviour could be observed without being seen it was an excellent mode of study. In Nhlangano, the female lecturers, some of the males and especially Leonard Nkambule, all seemed to agree that, as well as Science labs, it would be a really useful addition. Not only would it give the children a head start and be of benefit for studying child development, but it would of course be of practical help to the Mums on the campus. It could be used for demonstration lessons with the older children when the pre schoolers weren't around. I got quite excited at the prospect of introducing some handicapped children into the mix and some time later, I was reliably told, the suggestion was viewed favourably by the EU officials in Mbabane.

However, as Leonard's replacement, I was about to meet the most difficult Swazi to work with that I encountered during my time there. Yet again, I thought, here was a new, inexperienced, nominally HoD to initiate into the workings of the Education Department, the third in as many years. I thought wrong. He was not about to be initiated into anything, had not come to co-operate and had nothing to learn. He knew it all, or so he thought. Fair enough, that should reduce my workload. Dlamini, or the Dreaded Dlamini as I always named him in my thoughts, was a big, blustering, misogynist who was anxious never to display any lack of knowledge or competence, covering his insecurity by not delegating, letting nothing out of his own hands, never asking the members of the department their opinion or advice and bullying those around him. He was very firmly The Head and we were the underlings who needed to do as we were told. That included his long suffering wife and children whom he ruled with a rod of iron or the swish of a cane more likely. Unlike everyone else in our department, Dlamini was not even occasionally addressed by his first name and I can't recall what it was. I don't know where he arrived from. This was quite usual in my experience; people appeared and disappeared which probably had something to do with my lack of Siswati. I cannot imagine how he ever came to be involved with anything to do with young children. He had no empathy for them or women for that matter. I'm not even sure he had any rapport with secondary age children if his harsh treatment of his own is anything to go by. Judging from his subsequent career my guess is he must have been "moved sideways" from his previous job in usual Swazi fashion; sideways or upwards, especially if you had some status, never down and rarely out. No one ever seemed to get sacked, they were just moved from one unsuitable post to the next. Since he lacked the level of qualifications of those in his department under him, it was decided he'd better do the correspondence course in Education offered by UNISWA in Pretoria. This enabled him with not just the connivance but with the active encouragement of the Principal, to get help with his assignments from some of the other lecturers, especially Michael Oldridge the Maths and fellow ODA lecturer. It did not include those inferior creatures, the women lecturers of the Education Department. It did seem a little odd to appoint someone as HoD and then play catch-up but what did I know? The wisest move seemed to be to keep my head down and wait for better days.

He was also a religious fundamentalist who quoted God's word as though he had a direct line to the Almighty who would seem to be in perfect agreement with every opinion Dlamini held, however outrageous.

Since there was no cooperation with the rest of the department, I have no idea what went on in his classes but things finally came to a head when the collection, evaluation, collation and handing in of course results ready for the University was not done. A serious omission. Humiliated at being reprimanded by the Principal, Dlamini promptly came storming round, shouting and blamed me. It was all my fault; I had failed to carry out his instructions. When I protested that he had never given me any such instructions and, as Head, it was his responsibility to deal with the results anyway, he got very angry and abusive and called me a liar. Now a mild, "there seems to have been a misunderstanding or a bit of a mix up" I could have coped with and even helped him, but an emphatic, "You are a liar" proved to be the last straw in a fraught relationship. So I went to the Principal, demanded an apology and threatened to resign. That put the cat among the pigeons.

Vilakasi was visibly shaken. Women demanding apologies from Swazi men? Never. But ODA personnel insulted and resigning might be even worse. A bit of a misunderstanding, he said, a language problem. "Oh? So would he not mind being shouted at and called a liar and totally unjustly at that? "Well, cultural differences, you know and he would certainly sort it out. Just leave it with him." I had my doubts about that, but since my leave was just due and I didn't really want to resign, I did a bit of a climb down and agreed to leave it in his hands. Meanwhile, my standing among the women lecturers went up considerably. In any case, I wanted so much to be there when the pre school/observation classroom was built so, with at least that happy prospect in mind, I flew home for my inter contract leave to catch up on some parenting of my own.

When I returned a couple of months later, I learned to my astonishment that while I was away Vilakasi, the Principal had gone to the US on a term's scholarship and my bête noire, the Dreaded Dlamini was acting Principal. There he was, kicked upstairs while my back was turned! Not exactly what came to mind when Vilakasi said he would sort it out! To cap it all, one of Dlamini's first acts after his elevation to the seat of power, I was told, had been to put a red pencil line through the request for the preschool facility I was so keen on. I was devastated. My egotistical dream of leaving a lasting legacy gone. I was furious. I found it really hard to believe that he even had the power to make such a decision. Why had no one tried to stop him? I knew why of course. The name Dlamini, status, friends/relations in high places and a penis, sure-fire requisites for power in Swaziland. So, back to square one. Start again.

When Vilakasi returned from the US the Dreaded Dlamini did not resume his Headship of the Education Department. He disappeared; promoted to the headship of Mahamba Secondary School, I was told. That seemed a more suitable appointment. Some months later, the boys (and staff?) of Mahamba didn't agree with that evaluation and went on strike. I don't know the outcome of that but there was some talk that Dlamini had moved to a Headship in the Republic.

Although we didn't get a pre school facility, EEC did build a demonstration classroom with a one way glass observation wall. When it got to my turn to take a demonstration English lesson, the first thing that happened was a little hand shot up to tell me I had made a spelling mistake on the blackboard. A Swazi child actually telling a teacher she had got it wrong – which I had! It was just too good an opportunity to miss so I temporarily abandoned my prepared lesson to play 'find the mistake'. Sometimes I'd put words in the wrong place, make simple tense or spellings errors and sometimes, to fool them, had no mistake at all. Those not up to that level, just read the sentences out loud and I encouraged them to confer with their neighbour to decide what, if anything, was wrong and come to the board to put it right. With a bit of hamming it up I got them giggling and I was enjoying myself. Since it was a spur of the moment lesson, I had no follow up work to give them so I had to return to my original prepared material. The verdict of my students? The children were disrespectful!

It was only during my fourth or fifth year, with the help of my sympathetic new colleague, Ruby Dlamini, that we branched out and set our students a very basic task of observing a handicapped child of any kind in their home areas in addition to their usual child study project. This was totally new to them and the results proved very interesting. Most described children with a physical disability since this was the easiest to recognize, no doubt. Of the 150 studies undertaken, more than 80 described children who were born normal and then developed shorter or withered limbs. To me this sounded like polio – something that could so easily be prevented. Of the parents who were interviewed 30% said the children's disability was due to witchcraft.

We didn't as yet have any books or materials as to the different kinds of handicap and though Ruby and I approached a Catholic home for the handicapped to create some of our own material, we were angrily turned away. But at least our little survey got useful discussions going if nothing else. But that 30% result, that was a different problem. Persuading the families to get their children vaccinated was someone else's responsibility, thank goodness, and I didn't envy them the task. But with time and better knowledge, things could only improve, couldn't they?

In July 2016, 30 years later, The Times of Swaziland printed a piece about two children aged 16 and 8 who had been found at Etiyenia having been hidden from the world all their young lives due to their withered limbs. Edward Hlophe, the head of the family, says he was warned by government officials not to let the public see them "since it would paint a bad picture of Swaziland with the United Nations, especially if someone took a photo of them."

Well, at least it made the front page of The Times of Swaziland so I suppose that counts as progress of sorts. But this desire not to let the outside world know anything critical about Swaziland extends to the whole nation. Students going abroad on scholarship who spill the beans by telling the truth about what goes on at home are classified as traitors and vilified in parliament. But in truth, it is the people of Swaziland who know the least of what goes on in their own country since all forms of communication, the press, the radio, the TV and even the mobile phones and computer networks are owned by the king and heavily censored. Even the judiciary has to do his bidding while the whole country is made to hide behind this subterfuge of smoke and mirrors…

Only a question of time

Perhaps it was the Minister of Education himself or only one of his officials who got so enthusiastic about the company primary school at Big Bend. There were several in Swaziland established by international companies. They were intended in the first instance for the children of overseas workers though that entitlement now extended to all the workers of the company. They were endowed with good buildings, well paid staff, including some from overseas, modern equipment and small classes. Unlike many of the Swazi government primary schools. Nor were the children superglued to their seats and taught by the "repeat-after-me" method, a practice which might well have caused a mutiny amongst the European students who still made up a percentage of the classes.

Perhaps the enthusiasm on the part of the powers-that-be was aided by the effects of the good food and drink that the Big Bend Inn supplies on these occasions. Whatever the cause, the outcome was that the members of the Education Department, who were at that time four in number, were ordered to go and see how children should be taught and to pass this new-found wisdom on to their students.

Now if only, I thought, the results we were about to witness had been achieved in the kind of Swazi classroom I had once come across with seventy children, desks propped up by bricks, no books, no pencils, no doors, demoralised teachers and goats wandering in at will and eating the displays off the wall – then I would have been impressed! So would the rest of the department who knew perfectly well the discrepancies in achievement between the private and the public sector, the real causes of which would appear to have escaped the people in the Ministry up to now. But to oppose the directive would have been unthinkable. When the Ministry says go, you go!

So the four members of the Department prepared to abandon their classes for the day to seek enlightenment at Big Bend. It seemed a shame though, went the conversation in the college staff room, for the college combi to go all that way across the country with only the four members of the Education Department aboard. Much to my surprise, Mrs Msibi, Head of Home Economics demanded a place. Mrs Msibi was round and fierce and not to be denied. I had no idea she was interested in anything outside her own subject – food.

Then some other members of staff asked if they also could come on this visit of inspection. Impressed by their enthusiasm, Vilakasi informed Big Bend that, by popular demand, eleven members of staff would be arriving, which meant ten Swazis and me. An official programme was drawn up by Mr Parsons, the

Head of the school, lunch was ordered for us at Big Bend Inn for twelve noon, leaving us plenty of time to get there, and then we would see a demonstration of the children at work in the early afternoon before they went home at two thirty.

On the appointed day we were ready, with the exception of Mrs Msibi, to set off by eight thirty – well, near enough. A pleasant surprise since African timekeeping had a certain notoriety. It was a notoriety that Herbert Manzini, the deputy principal was determined to transform in the students at least. He expected them to be in class by nine o'clock sharp and to make sure they were, he made it his duty to patrol the walkway between the dormitories and the teaching block armed with a big cane. I never saw him use it though I did once see latecomers chased down the corridor by his Alsation. No other action seemed necessary.

I had just had an article published in the Times Ed. explaining African children's difficulty with timekeeping and thought it showed some insight. After all, I had written, most of the children didn't possess wristwatches nor was there any form of timekeeping in their huts. To get to school punctually and avoid punishment, they judged time by the length of shadows cast by physical features like certain rocks or trees and made quite sophisticated adjustments for the seasons. The trouble arose on

73

cloudy days when there was no sun.

There were no clouds today but Mrs Msibi still managed to keep us all waiting for a good ten minutes before she was spotted coming over the horizon, all chins quivering. A small cheer went up, we drove out of the gate, did a U turn and drove back in again – to get our tea money from the Principal, I was told.

Two hours later when we arrived in Manzini, the half way point, we stopped to spend it – at a bakery, at the Kentucky Fried Chicken, at a hamburger bar – all the places Nhlangano lacked. Then there were calls to relatives which simply had to be made and then shopping … all nerve wracking for a time-conscious European like myself. But then, I had never been to Big Bend and had no idea how far it was. Not even Dlamini, my then Head of Department and official leader of this jamboree seemed bothered in any way so I decided they must know what they're doing and left the worrying to him. Anyway, we still had an hour in hand to get there on time.

We drove on towards the Lowveldt, leaving the hills of the Middleveldt behind us to be replaced by flat fields of cotton, sugar cane and citrus orchards. It was all so interesting and new, I didn't really mind not being able to understand the conversations around me. I found Siswati a very difficult language, especially the clicks and hadn't got any further than the "Hello, I see you" greeting and even that wasn't very good. When we finally drove through some imposing looking gates, I looked at my wristwatch with a sigh of relief – ten minutes to twelve.

It was the mountains of oranges, lemons and grapefruit that gave it away. No bend of the river – no river even. No primary school, no welcoming hostelry. It swiftly dawned on me that we had arrived at a large packing station in the middle of citrus orchards. Totally bemused, I watched from the shelter of the combi while Mrs Msibi and one or two others climbed down and sent messengers scurrying in all directions to find a certain Swazi worker whom they obviously knew. After lengthy greetings and animated conversation, he referred them to a white overseer and I heard them ask if the company would make a donation of fruit for the college athletes who were taking part in the inter college games shortly.

Athletes? What athletes? I couldn't recall any athletes. Did they mean the rather lethargic group of women students I had seen running around the perimeter of the tennis courts with their long skirts flapping around their calves? Vilakazi put modesty before athletic prowess and wouldn't let them perform in shorts. Or did they mean the motley collection of men running around the dustbowl that passed for a football pitch – or both?

Surrounded as he was by Swazi women, the white

overseer opted for political correctness and told them they could fill a container with oranges with his blessing and then he fled.

A container? One of the Swazi labourers handed them a large packing box. Not exactly what they had in mind. They looked around. But of course! They had a container, a large one. The bus! And they set about filling and refilling the packing box with oranges and tipping them into the combi through an open window. Eager hands pushed the oranges under the back seat. When that was full, they tucked them under the other seats and along the gangway gradually carpeting the bus in pungent orange fruit. They looked and smelled gorgeous and so did the grapefruit stacked outside. When did I last taste a grapefruit? Certainly not after coming to Nhlangano where even the arrival of a few pockmarked local pears in the market was something of an event for me. So, after the initial shock of realising what was happening and realising also that we were likely to be here for some time, I got off the bus and bought myself a gunny sack of grapefruit.

Bowling along half an hour later, every time we drove up a slight incline, passengers in the back quickly had to lift their legs in unison like a row of chorus girls to avoid being swamped by a flood tide of rolling oranges. And downhill the process was reversed accompanied by helpless laughter. It wasn't till we pulled up at Big Bend Primary School at a quarter to three that the laughter suddenly dried up.

"Where on earth did you people get to?" the Head demanded with a face like thunder, "When we phoned they told us you'd left before nine."

Before I'd even quite stepped off the bus, he was addressing me directly, towering over me and I was shocked to realise that just because I was the only white face there, he assumed I was in charge. For once the Dreaded Dlamini didn't rush to assert his superior position as Head of Department leaving me to deal with the situation and I felt ten pairs of eyes boring into my back to see what I would do.

"We had to send the children home, you know," the Head rushed on without waiting for an answer and then delivered the final blow, "And we cancelled your lunches!"

This unexpected elevation to the dizzy heights of leader left me at a loss for some convincing lies especially as the bus was reeking strongly of oranges and he only had to step into it or even to look past me to know exactly why we were late. Kicking a couple of errant oranges out of view behind me, I stepped off the bus and shut the door.

"We had to stop a couple of times on the way," I said lamely looking very uncomfortable and clutching my stomach, "Quick, do you have a ladies?"

77

They rustled us up some sad looking sandwiches and marched us round the empty classrooms.

"Swazi teachers would have held the children back till the visitors arrived," said Mrs Msibi firmly. She was not an advocate of child centred education. Very un-Swazi, she thought.

It was already dark when we drove back into our college compound. At each house the cry went out, "Fetch a bucket!" and the oranges were scooped off the floor till the bucket could hold no more whereupon child, bucket and oranges would disappear up the garden path.

"Tambuti Citrus Company has generously donated an orange to each of our competing students," said Vilakazi proudly next day as he handed out the remaining ones, "And we must thank our teachers for taking the time to make it possible."

A Road Much Travelled

Every month, for more than forty years, it was said, Mrs Lord had packed her gear, left their hardware store in Nhlangano in the reluctant hands of Mr Lord, saddled up her horse and set off before sunrise to travel 160km over the mountains to play tennis in Mbabane. Why, I wondered, did she make the gruelling journey to play in the capital when there was a thriving local club up the hill in Hlatikulu with all the expatriate amenities which went with it? Was there something wrong with the local expatriate community or perhaps, her relationship with the unfortunate Mr Lord? Was there a tennis playing lover waiting for a match on the courts of Mbabane? I have no idea.

In those pre 1970's days, any traveller seeking the bright lights and fleshpots of the sophisticated north had only two ways to get to the capital of Swaziland from our area in the far south of Shiselweni. Both of them meant a long, winding, tedious and sometimes dangerous journey on dirt roads. One over the mountains to the north over Kabuta and Spiphoneni, the other west over Mankyane and Malkerns. Mrs King chose the northern route. The cricketing fraternity chose the western.

They often broke their journey en route to cricket matches up north (or, more likely, on the way back after too much celebrating) at the half-way point to sample the hospitality of Miss Tyson, the publican, at the Mankyane Arms. It was alleged that Maggie Tyson had been an ATA pilot during the second world war in Europe, ferrying replacement planes or delivering new ones, to wherever they were needed. You could easily imagine her ample frame in a leather suit with helmet and goggles. More often than not, you didn't need much imagination. If she wasn't around, regular guests would stroll over to the yard and look for a couple of legs in filthy dungarees sticking out from under a clapped out old van and there would be Maggie, spanner in hand, attached to the end of them. If that failed and she really was away, guests helped themselves at the bar and left the money on the counter. Those staying overnight, the enterprising ones anyway, heated their own bathwater. Up in the cold of the mountains, a hot bath to wash off the red dust of the roads was a luxury not to be missed. So guests willingly kept the water flowing hot by feeding the wood stove in the bathroom from the pile of logs Maggie left ready. If you just stretched out, you could do this without actually leaving the comfort of your bath.

It stands to reason, of course, that between these two mountain ranges there was a valley, a deep one, also two major rivers running through, the Usuto and the Mbuluzi flowing down to Mozambique. Sometime in the thirties, the Howard family bought some land half way down to the floor of one of the valleys and bravely attempted to farm it. Anyone who tried taming the bush to farm also had to build their own road to get to it, coat and compact it with murram (mud) in the dry winter and probably watch the heavy summer rains wash it all away exposing the rock and flints that ripped your tyres. In addition, if you wanted that new fangled contraption, the telephone, when it finally arrived in the district in the mid thirties, you had to put up your own poles. Of course the preponderance of heavy summer storms in this part of Africa with their dramatic flashes of lightning meant the workings regularly blew a fuse or, occasionally, the coloured wires might get stolen and be transformed into beautiful African woven baskets. For the Howards, it was comparatively simple to let their Austin 7 roll down the incline of thirty or forty plus degrees, but a lot harder trying to zigzag up again without sliding backwards, hitting potholes and ending in the bushes. They had very few visitors.

When you did make it down to the valley, there was the problem of the rivers to cross. During the dry seasons, on the smaller crossings, the powers-that-be had built concrete platforms on the riverbed just about wide enough to take an ox wagon or a car. At other times you had to judge for yourself how far up the chassis the water could safely come before the car stalled. Or you could take a chance, accelerating through at speed like a power boat except that you were driving across the flow so, instead of sending a wash to the back of the vehicle, the full force of the water hit you sideways on, sending waves crashing on your windows, obscuring your view of the track ahead. On the wider rivers, a raft ferried men, beasts and vehicles across. It's said it sometimes failed to make it when the load was too heavy, like the time returning cricketers gave a lift in their bakkies to a group of stranded Swazi princesses with their heads decked in the red loerie feathers denoting their rank. Rank didn't save them as the raft slowly sank, but luckily the cricketers did. But things were about to change.

In 1979 McAlpines started on the first tarmac road to be built through the valley. Equipment and workmen were shipped out from Britain; mountains were modified, encroaching rocks blown up, rivers bridged, gradients lowered and bush tamed. Due to sanctions, they even shipped out prefabricated housing from Europe for the workers. It took almost four years and millions and millions of pounds but at the end of it all, by 1983, one could drive in smooth comfort and be in the capital, Mbabane, in two hours, just about, barring the meandering cows. Such excitement! It opened new vistas. There would be an era of economic prosperity for the farmers around Nhlangano with faster access to markets and better prices; we were no longer so cut off from the cultural life of the north; we could get to the airport and the big fashion shops and even a cinema, not to mention the Chinese restaurant! I could fetch David home from school at Waterford every other weekend more quickly and enjoy some family life. It was all so wonderful. But that was before Demoina.

People spoke of Agatha, Betty and Cecilia, previous cyclones I'd never heard of but the dreaded Demoina is the one I shall never forget. Hurricanes erupt furiously, wreak havoc and are gone. They get boy's names like Freddy and George and Henry. But a cyclone, a miserable, hefty amount of rain, which nags on and on and on and won't move and won't stop, that is considered female. So, six months after the completion of the road, in January 1984 Demoina arrived from the Indian ocean spreading havoc over a vast area from Mozambique to Natal and the Transvaal with Swaziland in the middle. Her rotating winds had lessened, replaced by solid sheets of rain which fell hour after hour, all day, all night, all the next day and the next, never stopping. The view from the windows was obscured by curtains of water, ditches overflowed until they were one with the roads while pastures turned into sudden lakes drowning the unsuspecting cattle and ruining the harvest ready crops. New waterfalls splashed down the mountainsides, became raging torrents, licked the foundations of whole villages of clay and wattle houses until piece by piece, they slid down the hillsides, crumbled and were swept away, some tragically with their owners. People tried desperately to rescue the few bits of furniture they had, their chairs and tables, their cooking pots and trunks but it was difficult to stay on your feet and keep your balance in the slippery mud and, in any case, saving the children had to take priority. Many lost their lives.

Rivers rose, some over 70 feet, and gathering strength, they gauged their banks and toppled trees turning them into battering rams slamming into the bridges over and over until they too collapsed with the onslaught. Altogether more than a hundred were damaged or destroyed. But surely, we thought, our beautiful new road, our fully tarmacked road would be immune. The water would run over its solid surface into those deep gullies and continue down the mountain sides. We thought wrong. Like uprooting the riverside trees, if Demoina couldn't penetrate the solid tarmacadam, she would dig underneath the gentle curves and gradients of the road, lift huge sections of it and fling them down into the valley or float them down to the level below. Gentle or ferocious, the result was the same. No more road.

So that was why, whenever I had to go to the capital to fetch David home from school, the choice was between crossing into South Africa, driving north and back into Swaziland at the Oshoek border or the old route over the mountain tops, over Mankyanne and Malkerns. But there was no Maggie Tyson to welcome me, no Mankyane Inn anymore. The concrete bases of the rivers were back in use again as were the steamrollers flattening the murram – accepting that it was in the nature of things that the annual rains would wash it away; accepting that year upon year, like sowing and reaping, the process would have to be repeated again.

The Mission

The well appointed American house in the village, didn't quite fit in with my picture of missionaries. That was more in the style of Peter Carlton the incumbent Anglican parson who pedalled his way around the village on an ancient bike which could be heard from quite a distance squealing loudly for lubrication. But even he didn't reach the saintly heights of the Kjaers, (Keers) an elderly Danish couple out at Nzongomani Mission, a remote station reached only by driving through Shiselweni Forest. They had built their mission house themselves, stone by stone and next to it, a simple primary school. I made their acquaintance rather dramatically when I inadvertently acquired a Swazi "daughter". It all came about because I couldn't wash my clothes in a bucket.

When I first got to the campus, I was given a very small furnished bungalow. There was no washing machine or room for one, no bath either, only a small shower and a tiny galley kitchen. The only way I could think to wash my clothes and household stuff was at the cold water tap outside using a large bucket; a bit of a come down from just throwing everything into a machine and going off to do something more interesting. My futile efforts at hand washing generally drew an audience and provided lots of local entertainment until eventually one of the other lecturers took pity and found a suitable woman to help me. And so Noma entered my life.

She had the most amazing energy, throwing everything into the yard whenever she came, scrubbing every surface in sight, washing, ironing and even gardening. It seemed too good to last and of course, it was. Early one morning, on a day I wasn't expecting Noma, there was a banging on my door and I found a young girl standing there with a baby slung on her back.

"My mother, my mother," she kept crying hysterically.

"Your mother?" I said puzzled, "There's no mother here."

"My mother, she works for you."

"Noma? What's the matter with Noma?"

"She's dead. My mother is dead." and she got quite hysterical again.

Evidently Noma had suffered from very high blood pressure which had taken its inevitable toll. But that was only the start of the family's problems. By Swazi Law and Custom, women had no property rights and although Noma's husband had deserted the family and contributed nothing to their upkeep for the past thirteen years, as soon as she was dead, he was throwing the children out of their house and claiming it as his own. It was little more than a shanty really but at least Noma had somehow built it herself with her own earnings from scrubbing and cleaning. And then there was the problem of the ten month old baby. It belonged to the young girl on the doorstep who looked, and indeed was, not a day over fifteen. She had finally got a place to study at the High School, a much sought after prize. Only about 25% of the school population were able to go on after primary school. With mother dead and no one else to pay the school fees or take care of ten month old Baby Howie, how could she hope to get any sort of qualification?

The father of the baby?

He didn't want to know.

At that point I should perhaps have given her some money and pointed her in the direction of … direction of what? There was no safety network as far as I was aware apart from family and as she said she had none except a younger brother here and a sister in Soweto somewhere, the problem remained on my doorstep, so to speak. Noma had only been working for me a few months but something had to be done for this homeless, weeping girl and her baby so I reluctantly took it upon myself to try to sort out the mess.

This resulted in my being summoned before a meeting of the local Chief and Elders to discuss the fate of my "daughter" Busi. I say "discuss" whereas in reality I had no idea what was being said by this group of very elderly men, mostly in national dress with the usual pom-poms slung across their bare chests, sitting in a circle and talking in siSwati for what seemed like hours without any reference to me at all, not so much as a glance. However, very surprisingly, the outcome was the children were allowed to stay in their house. I didn't realise at the time quite what a seismic change from Swazi Law and Custom that represented. Now the remaining problems were school fees, maintenance and most important – the baby.

That's when I approached the saintly Kjaers. Between them they had brought up and educated 135 abandoned Swazi children so perhaps, I thought, just perhaps, they could temporarily take on number 136 until Busi was in a position to resume caring for him herself. Alas, they said, they were now almost in their eighties and felt unable to deal with any more young children. However, I could try their companion Mission out on the road to Gege run by their colleague Miss Wibelo. She was only 65! She was also about to say no but then she saw the baby, in his sling, peeping over Busi's shoulder and she fell in love. One look at this lovely bright little boy was enough to melt Miss Wibelo's heart and she adored him from then on. Eventually I got grants from Save the Children and a local church which, with a little top up input from me, took care of Busi's finances so things were more or less resolved, I thought, over optimistically as usual. In fact my troubles were just beginning.

Busi told us that Robert, a very personable young man who worked in the local supermarket was the father of her baby. Apart from sneaking a good look at him as I did some shopping, that was going to be the end of my involvement. However, when the Reverent Gjosund, yet another Dane, who ran the other affiliated mission, heard the rumours going round, as they do only too readily in such a small place, he was furious and vehemently denied that Robert, his special prodigy, could possibly have fathered a baby. Since he was himself a father of five I would have thought he might have worked that possibility out by now. It seemed to bother him a great deal more than the fate of this young girl who had been the victim, at thirteen, of what was classified as statutory rape. I hadn't been aware that there was any such legislation until I was told King Sobhuza had initiated it back in the 1920s. I doubt many of the population had heard of it either. Not Noma or Busi, I presume, since they had cared for the baby all this time as a matter of course, irrespective of his parentage. Had Noma not died, that is how things would have continued. Underage pregnancies and illegitimate babies were common. According to UN statistics, one in three Swazi girls between thirteen and eighteen had been subjected to sexual violence or abuse, mainly from family. That was probably an underestimate. A culture of silence and respect for one's elders meant most girls didn't report the offence which they often regarded as shameful but not as shameful as disloyalty for the family's name. Rather than reporting assaults or rapes to the authorities, the extended family was inclined to sort matters out themselves, (traditionally known as tibi tendlu), with no outside intervention, particularly reports to the police. Given that the voices of authority in the extended family were men who claimed all rights over their womenfolk, including assault, I didn't hold out much hope of justice for them. Nevertheless, I had the feeling that I was being fed information by the college sisterhood because, being an expatriate and a guest in the country, it was more likely to have an effect despite my being a woman. They might have had a point.

The Reverent Gjosund had several handsome young men in his ministry, but he had special plans for Robert whom he was grooming to take a course in the seminary over the border in Ermalo with a view to a pastorship or perhaps even taking over his own ministry eventually. The police had other ideas and took away Robert's passport, which was amazing given the usual police reaction of dismissal of any complaints by women. Not that we had lodged any complaint in the first place. Did they know something we didn't? Was there another agenda? No one, least of all Busi and I, had wanted matters to become so complicated. All we wanted was for her to get an education so she could get a decent job and get on with her life but we were up against a lot of powerful opposition. Twice I was called away from work, summoned by the school because there had been objections to "my daughter's" presence there and demands that she be thrown out. I guessed rightly they originated from Robert's father who unfortunately, happened to be a headmaster in the neighbouring district. Twice I fought her corner, quoting the Girl's and Women's Protection Act of 1920 of King Sohbusa and pointing out angrily why those particular objectors wanted her out, to vanish, for reasons of their own prestige, whereas all we wanted was some peace and quiet. Neither would throwing her out alter the facts of the case. She was allowed to stay.

Robert disappeared from the supermarket and things quietened down for a few months. Then Miss Wibelo's fellow missionaries from Ermelo just happened to make one of their regular social visits to Swaziland and met the delightful little Howie and of course the story of his background came out. What also came out was that Robert, the father, was at that moment happily studying at their seminary in Ermolo, calm as you please with no mention of the trouble he was in back home. And how had he managed to get over the border without a passport? Someone had mysteriously acquired a second one for him, we presumed, or perhaps bought back the original. And how was it that Rev. Gjosund, in full knowledge of the facts and the strict entrance qualifications the seminary required, which would certainly exclude the impregnation of a 13 year old and the rejection of his responsibilities as the father had, nevertheless, covered up and got him in there to train for the ministry? Questions needed to be asked and they duly were. Consequences needed to follow and they did, none of which interested or involved me. It was hardly Busi's fault that Robert was thrown out of the seminary. What did involve me was the unpleasant, incessant pressure meted out to Busi subsequently in revenge. The malicious persecution by all concerned finally overwhelmed her till she could take no more. She disappeared one night together with her younger brother, joined her sister in Soweto (I presume) and was never seen again. Not the outcome I had hoped for, especially for the baby.

Some time later I received an unexpected invitation for tea from the Kjaers and when I got there they both thanked me profusely and told me God had sent me in answer to their prayers. I had no idea what they were talking about and denied being sent by anyone, human or divine. But they were adamant. The Rev. Gjosund had been a disgrace to their ministry for years, they said, ruining those poor young men until I came along doing God's work and exposing him. That was news to me. I neither knew nor cared about the Reverent's sexual orientation or behaviour and felt that young Swazi men were more than capable of looking after themselves. It was the young girls who needed protection. However, it did shed new light on the reaction of the police.

Up until then, my only experience of the police had been the usual near end of month speed traps when funds were low and police pay day a while off. It didn't take me long to figure out that it was useless to argue about my speed or that I would actually be handed a ticket so I kept just enough in my purse to satisfy both parties and proceed on my way. Then Robin, the helpful man from the Casino, with whom I was now very friendly, had his car stolen. Surprisingly, it was recovered by the South African police over the border and returned to him. It did sport a few bullet holes where they'd shot at the driver but at least he got it back unlike many owners of more prestigious, expensive cars.

Staying at the Casino was an insurance inspector who had been sent from the Republic to investigate why so few cars recovered by the South African police were reunited with their Swazi registered owners. The explanation he found was that the Swazi pound for recovered vehicles was somewhere remote in the bush with a rather small notice on the gate, the size of a postcard, stating, as the law demanded, that cars not reclaimed within a month would be deemed to be abandoned and sold off. In consequence, not only were poorly paid Swazi policemen driving around in BMWs and Mercs, but some of the cars had been traced to Zambia and Zimbabwe. One even made it to Australia. As a result of his findings the insurance man expected the senior Swazi police to take action against the group running this scam but the opposite applied. He was P.Id, (declared a prohibited immigrant) escorted to the border and forbidden to set foot in Swaziland again. It was an option used on more than one occasion by the Swazis to dispose of uncomfortable truths or disputes and it saved a lot of manpower and paperwork. QED.

Much the same tactics were used when women came to the station as a last resort, to report being beaten up by their husbands or boyfriends. They were sent home again and told to be better wives in future. Mothers who complained that their young daughters were being sexually exploited by their teachers got the same treatment. Go home. What did arouse the Swazi Constabulary into action was any whiff of

95

homosexuality. It was against the law at that time but if detected, the punishment was not on the scale of the Ugandan government law where, even in 2014, life imprisonment resulted or Zimbabwe where, since 2006, the mere holding of hands or hugging between males could mean a custodial sentence. In Swaziland the negative consequences were more societal. Gay men were subject to serious social discrimination with chiefs refusing land allocation, evicting them from their homes or banishing them from the area as well as the general disapprobation of the rest of society especially the Christians. Un-Swazi and un-Christian was the general verdict. But since the deterioration of people's rights in the past two decades and the clampdown on any forms of protest by labelling everything which was not to the liking of the royal family 'terrorism', it has given the Army and the Police unbridled rights to assault just about anyone. Having a different sexual orientation, while still mainly unacceptable, has been overshadowed by the general brutality and human suffering that is now let loose in Swaziland.

A Mixed Bunch

For such a tiny town of only four thousand or so inhabitants in the 80s, Nhlangano had more than its fair share of different nationalities. In the late seventies and early eighties it was heavily augmented by foreign McAlpine road construction workers, but once they were gone the town returned to its sleepy but no less cosmopolitan self.

For a start, Evelyn Baring, the local secondary school, as well as having the local Swazi teachers, hosted quite a few expatriates like Scottish Robert Kirk, the technical and woodwork teacher of many year's standing: the Sivers, also Scottish, who both taught Science: some Belgium and Canadian VSO (or the national equivalent) teachers; American Peace Corps workers; a couple of expatriate wives, a Zambian teaching Maths and Joyce, the Ghanaian wife of the local vet who taught Home Economics and kept the bowling fraternity well supplied with scones and other goodies. Yao, her husband, as well as tending the local animals, was also very useful for tending us locals in an emergency in the absence of other medical help if the need arose.

CDC's Forestry Commission employed several British ODA contract workers in their management accompanied by their wives and families. Canadian Overseas Aid projects like water development and

97

agriculture added to the number, as did the Dutch volunteer doctors working up at at Hlatikulu hospital who sometimes made it down the hill to join in some activity or other. And one mustn't leave out the expatriate staff of the very important (and unlikely) local Casino/hotel, established to entice the gamblers from over the border where gambling was forbidden at that time; the German chef, the South African management and a few of the croupiers. Occasionally they were joined by the casino's debt collector chasing those gamblers who somehow believed the tables would make their fortune and didn't know when to stop. In contrast, there were several Danish missionaries scattered around the region and last, but not least, were the ODA appointed lecturers, four at one time, including me, who were helping the new EEC funded Ngwane Teacher Training College get on its feet. All these people were resident on a temporary basis, passing on their skills, training local Swazis to take their place before returning to their various countries.

I particularly remember Andreas the chef at the Casino. The menu he produced was top class so it was a mystery to me what this master of his craft was doing in such a small, unimportant dorp. But more of that later.

There was also a charming Canadian couple with Water Aid. Canadians were not allowed by their government to venture over the border into Apartheid South Africa which proved a very serious problem when their first baby was due and the road through the valley had been washed away. The only way for them to get to the hospital in Mbabane, the capital, was by the small aircraft belonging to the owner of the supermarket. And then there were those two teachers…

We hardly knew the Belgian teachers so we were startled, to say the least, to have a weeping Birgit come up to us in the ablution block of the camp in Kruger Park begging for help. Robin and I, who were an item by this time, had decided to snatch a week-end away for some animal spotting, driven some six hours north to the park and were staying in one of the rondavels inside the safety perimeter fence. Next to them was a field for those intrepid souls who preferred to bring their own tent. Although South African game parks were very comfort conscious, in this particular camp you still had to use central kitchens, wash- houses and toilet blocks and it was in one of these, I forget which, that the fateful meeting took place.

She had been stuck here, she said, for the last three days with only a tiny tent (just big enough to crawl into) while her husband drove off to Nelspruit, the nearest town, to get the car repaired, he said, and hadn't come back. Naturally enough, surrounded as we were by wild animals inhabiting an area about the size of Wales, it was forbidden to venture outside the perimeter fence on foot. To get news of him she needed transport. There were no telephones in the park and she was running out of food but most of all she was worried about him. So we packed the tent and weeping wife into the car and set off to find the nearest ranger post. The only means of communication with the world outside the park at that time, was by radio and they duly contacted the police at Nelspruit to see if there had been any reports of a road accident or a mugging perhaps? There were none. We reported him as a missing person. All we could do now was wait. It was mid afternoon before news came in that he had been found – in the local jail. He had sold the car, gone on a drinking binge and was picked up lying dead drunk in a bar somewhere. Then it all came out. We were dealing with an alcoholic who had no scruples, it seemed, about leaving his wife to the mercy of African wildlife. What on earth did he think she was going to do abandoned, without any transport, inside a perimeter fence in the biggest game park in Africa? He obviously couldn't think beyond the next bottle.

The next step was for us to take her all the way to Nelspruit, some two hours drive away, and find some means of getting them both home. But which home? Home to Belgium Birgit decided. Enough was enough. This was one humiliation too many and she would leave him and fly straight to Brussels. We contacted the airline. She had enough money for the flight and he could make his own arrangements. And with that, we left her in the capable hands of the SA police and drove back to Kruger to enjoy what was left of our holiday.

Wandering through Nhlangano a couple of days after our return, I thought I saw a familiar figure but it couldn't be, could it? It could. It was Birgit.

"I could not leave him" she pleaded, "I luff him!"

Luff or no luff, a short time afterwards things came to a head. The school threw him out for drunkenness and since he showed no signs of leaving of his own accord, the Belgium Attache turned up from the capital with an escort who made sure he was put on a flight to Brussels before he did any more damage to the reputation of Belgium. We could only hope he sought help and ended worthy of the love she gave him but I doubt it.

There were also some long established Swazi mixed race or Eurafrican residents of Nhlangano, going back several generations in some cases. They were generally called "coloureds" in Southern Africa which was not a name I approved of. Did that make the rest of us colourless? Well, the college staff did refer to the white population of South Africa as 'the

Blanks' a reference to "sleg vor blankes" (only for whites) notices everywhere across the border. Here, among the Eurafricans there were the Carmichaels, Wes and Ivy. She kept a small cafe and he became the Sheriff. I have no idea what that entails but it sounds suitably Wild West. There were also other traditional mixed race families like the Henwoods, Bennetts, Adams, Nunns and Furtardos. Not being part of the traditional Swazi system, they could not be granted land tenure by the local chief who allocated the use of SNL (Swazi Nation Land) only to the male heads of Swazi families under his jurisdiction. Instead, they ran cafes, shops, hairdressers, bottle stores, chemists or garages though they could buy private land available and often did very well. The Henwoods for instance had a lovely daughter, Karen, who also went to Waterford like David. They tended to marry mixed race partners or preferably Europeans judging by the number of such couplings. This was understandable knowing the rights any Swazi husband could assume over his wife and children. Best avoided. Theirs was a subtle relationship with the rest of the community.

Unlike many compliant Swazi women, the mixed race wives of Nhlangano were confident and strong, one or two verging on the aggressive. Given their ambiguous positions in society, they had to fight their corner. One young woman, furious at finding her European boyfriend had taken up with another, set about trashing his car with a hammer. Unfortunately, it wasn't his car. It belonged to his employer who was none too pleased when he saw the result. The prize for aggression though has to go to Ellen Furtardo. Her husband Tony, of mixed Portuguese and African ancestry, ran a local hardware store and their daughter Isabel was married briefly to an American Peace Corps ski instructor (not a profession much in demand in Southern Africa). Ellen seemed to make a career out of quarreling with just about everyone. It ended tragically, so I'm told, when gentle giant Tony finally snapped, shot her dead and then turned the gun on himself.

Somewhat less dramatic, after Robin and I had decided to live together and moved into the town, was our young Eurafrican next door neighbour Harry and his wife. We suspected he and his friends were doing something nefarious after we were woken in the night by a series of explosions like the rat-a-tat of a machine gun coming from his drive and saw his car well ablaze and the windows spewing exploding glass everywhere. At least, we'd thought it was his up to that point but he didn't seem unduly concerned about this conflagration. "Burning the evidence," we said to each other and we weren't far wrong. But sometime later worse was to follow.

However, dubious activities weren't just the prerogative of the Swazi population. Wedged between Marxist Mozambique and sanction squeezed South Africa, little Swaziland was wide open for sanction busting, misusing grants or just being a kosher address for all kinds of exports which certainly hadn't originated there. France would have to have been several layers deep in wine if they had also produced the amount of bottles with French labels that passed through Swaziland from the RSA to other parts of Africa and beyond.

Goods just needed to be in Swaziland long enough to get the right stamp for further travel. Sometimes this amounted to just a few hours, especially for live stock. One such case consisted of pedigree sheep wanted for breeding in Kenya. One each of Romney Marsh, South Down, Cape Fat tail, a Merino stud ram and an Angora goat were railed some seven hundred miles from the Karroo to the Swazi border, bused to the nearest sheep farm, inspected within the hour and passed by the local vet, issued with valid Swazi export licenses, crated up, each in a special box and bused and trained a further 200 or so miles to Johannesburg on their way to Nairobi. Unfortunately when they arrived at Jan Smuts airport, the flight was delayed indefinitely and the place was swarming with reporters and police much to the alarm of the animals' minders. It seemed a rather excessive reaction to a bit of minor sanction busting, they thought. But the large police presence wasn't interested in the crated animals. It was the famous film star Diana Dors everyone was waiting for, sanction busting on her own account, I think, against the wishes of Equity. The sheep were in good company.

Absconding with government subsidies was also a local pastime. There were the two one-eyed Irishmen and their furniture manufacturing business followed by some white Zimbabweans trying to turn the same premises into a chipboard manufacturing factory but more of that later. Several white Zimbabweans came to Nhlangano to set up a tobacco growing enterprise which some suspected was a cover for illegal overseas arms trading though it was unclear at this stage, which side was being armed. Speculation was rife mainly because one of their number, a young Italian, who obviously knew nothing whatsoever about tobacco growing but a great deal about weapons, was the son of one of the world's most famous firearm manufacturers -Beretta. The list of dodgy doings is long.

At independence in 1968, there had been an exit of many of the South African residents of Shiselweni, the southernmost province of Swaziland, especially the Boers, possibly fearing reprisals which never happened. With the lapse of extradition treaties when the Republic left the Commonwealth in 1961, many anti-apartheid South Africans and ANC refugees had moved over the border seeking welcome sanctuary in the black kingdom. That though, altered somewhat after 1980 when ANC tactics in the Republic became more militant. Pressure was applied to Swaziland by the South African apartheid regime to renounce their allegiance to the ANC by the promise of land they had once owned 100 years ago. The incorporation of the KaNwane bantustan would double Swaziland's size and give them an outlet to the sea.. This land would be theirs they were promised if their erstwhile friends, the "terrorists" sheltering in the kingdom could be "dealt with" and cleared from the country. The Swazis took the bait.. ANC houses in Manzini were bombed and various kidnappings, murders and shoot outs took place forcing the ANC to move its activities further north to Lusaka. The promise of the land was dropped. They had betrayed their friends for nothing. In Nhlangano there were whispered rumours about the bodies of ANC sympathisers taken secretly over our local Mahamba border post in the middle of the night. We didn't believe it. Such things didn't happen in our idyllic, peaceful little corner. Just how naive can one be?

Of the White Swazis still living in Nhlangano, almost all were of British or South African ancestry. The most prominent were the McSeveney family who owned Skonkwane, the one and only supermarket in the town until OK Bazaars moved in. Young Jimmy ran the store while old Charlie McSeveney was in charge of the Native Recruitment Office finding labour for South African mines until he retired and then re-lived his wartime experiences over and over for anyone who would listen. Young Jimmy's ambition to run his modest store on the lines of the big players included owning a small plane to drop flyers over the countryside announcing the latest bargains. He did once try to fly it himself, misjudged the time for the distance he flew and only got back as darkness was falling. Since the landing strip in Nhlangano was only a farmer's field with a windsock and white painted markers he couldn't find the place to land. In the absence of any of today's means of communication and unable to utilize a radio signal, all he could do was fly round and round till some of the locals realized his difficulty and lined up their car headlights on the landing strip to get him down.

Some of the older residents remembered the time in the sixties when they were sometimes called out to shine their headlights through the windows at Hlatikulu hospital operating theatre when the generators packed up. Since Jimmy was now reluctant to fly himself ever again, Robin, retook his license and did the job for him. Really it was only for the joy of flying again. It didn't approach the thrill of flying his beloved wartime Spitfire as a fighter pilot in the Italian campaign but at least he only littered the countryside with paper, not anything more lethal. It also proved useful to fetch some young visitors, friends of my children, from the airport at Matsapha. The Jo'burg flight touched down a little late and since the airport could not function in the dark and shut down at 5.30pm, Robin had to push to the head of the immigration queue, fish the youngsters out, throw their luggage into the Cessna and get the authorities to reopen the airport so that he could take off to fly home while he could still see the landmarks below before it got too dim. Not an experience those youngsters would ever forget!

To catch their homeward flight meant I had to drive them to the airport on our badly damaged road. I was very nervous about this, so I made them all get out and walk safely over the really bad, washed away part at the sharp corner with the sheer, unguarded drop. I'd seen too many wrecks at the bottom of the cliff. If the car was going to join them, being the sole occupant, at least I'd have a chance of jumping out – or not.

Robin had spent more than 30 years trying to develop and wrest a modest living from a remote farm in the mountains near Hlatikulu about eleven miles from Nhlangano. In early 1983 when he finally decided to give up the struggle and sell, he was surprised to have the courtiers of the Queen Regent, Ndlovokasi Dzeliwe, the supreme head of the nation after King Sobhuza's death, turn up and offer to buy it on her behalf. They said she wanted to have somewhere quiet and remote, away from the quarrels and intrigues of the court and the farm certainly fitted that bill, so Robin sold it to her. Unfortunately she never made it away from the quarrels and intrigues. First Mabandla, the reforming PM was replaced by Prince Bhekimpi against Dzeliwe's wishes and then in August there was a palace coup. She was deposed and briefly kept under house arrest and the farm remained unoccupied in limbo for some years, quietly mouldering until she died. We think that some years later it was in the hands of another royal prince although we couldn't find any record of ownership in the Swaziland Land Registry and concluded it had joined that vast secret acreage in the hands of Tibyo used for patronage with no questions asked.

A few older people stayed on after their retirement like ex-teachers Molly and Ken Lapping. His brother, Douglas Lapping, was still going strong at the age of 74 as the only GP holding the fort as far as the Mozambique border to the east and the South African to the west. As well as having a clinic in town, he had set up a surgery in an abandoned cowshed on his farmland a few miles out. Empty beer bottles lined the shelves waiting to be filled with obnoxious medicines. They had to taste awful, he said, or his Swazi patients didn't believe it was doing them any good. He once saw me staring aghast at a stack of large yellow plastic jerry-cans labelled "Penicillin, for the use of cattle only" when I knew he didn't have any – cattle that is.

"It's just as good for people, you know," he said calmly, "And a damn sight cheaper."

Sundays were sacrosanct, kept free for Church, bowls at the club and a bottle of wine or even two. Nevertheless, if there was an emergency he would drop everything and go and attend to it, cursing as he went and leaving us bowlers floundering without a full team in mid match unlike the cricket team which had been known to get a convict or two out of jail to make up their side.

He was also the emergency doctor for the local Holiday Inn Casino which sometimes raised a few eyebrows. On one occasion he was called out after a Sunday game and a couple of bottles of wine and because he didn't have his stethoscope with him he put his ear to the prone patient's chest and dozed off, snoring gently. The patient had hysterics but the bowlers quite understood.

It was hard to reconcile the feeble figure shrunken

into his baggy trousers, food stains down his crisp white shirt and slurred speech after the latest little stroke with one of the amazingly courageous medical officers responsible for evacuating every last man of a defeated army in Burma before the advancing Japanese. His own luck ran out when the last means of escape was torpedoed out of the water forcing the few who were stranded to struggle hundreds of miles on foot through enemy occupied jungle territory and even more hostile mountains into present day Bangladesh. All this I got from other people. Douglas never talked about the war or his MBE. Nor did he talk about his attempt to publicize the dangers of asbestosis when he worked for the Havelock asbestos mines, a standpoint which lost him his job but gained Nhlangano a GP

In an old planters bungalow in the middle of town lived Taffy whose maiden name, Baragwanath was famous all over southern Africa and beyond. Baragwanath Hospital in Jo'burg is the biggest in the whole of Africa, established in 1941 by the British colonial powers to treat its WWII war wounded. Taffy was the widow of Auguste Language who had been the local lawyer. As far as Auguste was concerned, when people were unable to pay for his legal services, reluctant to take livestock in lieu which needed feeding and cleaning, he had sometimes taken goods instead, littering his yard with strange objects. Once there was even a redundant fire hydrant last used in the London blitz! How such things found their way to the other side of the world is a complete mystery.

Then there was retired farm manager Harry Lagerwahl whose Danish wife Lilimore had a stroke and made a partial recovery which, unfortunately left her unable to communicate in English, her second language. Since Harry knew no Danish, the poor lady eventually had to be shipped off to Denmark to live with her brother, the only one capable of understanding her. But once they were gone, and others too, the place emptied of elderly white Swazis. Gradually, it also emptied of foreign workers and aid personnel but that didn't stop Nhlangano thriving and almost doubling in size within the next 20 years.

Much of that success is down to people like my colleagues at Ngwane Teacher Training College. They were the Swazis I got to know best, apart from my students, especially the women, who welcomed me warmly into their sisterhood. They came mostly from other, more sophisticated, northern parts of Swaziland, were educated and intelligent and taught me about some of the chauvinist rules and regulations imposed on them by Swazi men. Let me hasten to add the majority of lecturers, male and female, had stable, civic, Christian marriages, the emphasis being on the Christian.

112

My colleague Eliza Shongwe was a widow with three children whose husband had been killed in a traffic accident in the Republic. Far from attracting help and sympathy for their plight, the position of Swazi widows was made unbelievably worse. Under Swazi Law and Custom, not only should they wear black full mourning for at least two years until a special cleansing ceremony released them from that obligation, but they should also be taken over by their late husband's brother as a junior wife (kungena). In polygamous households, all the wives would be taken over and if more than one brother died, their wives would be taken over as well, not to mention the children and all the family's worldly goods. Since the widows have the status of children, no one offers them any choice in the matter. They have no rights of inheritance and because only men have access to leases of Swazi Nation land, all too often they can be left with no proper support or even the ability to grow food for themselves and their children. Despite the various clauses in the 2005 constitution and all the international treaties Swaziland has signed regarding the rights of women and the protection of children, none have been implemented. Even now, it is not unusual for the paternal relatives of the deceased to come and take away all household items, grab any property and evict the bereaved family.

The rationale for this behaviour in traditional polygamous homesteads seems to be that the widow or widows should retreat to the seclusion of the special mourning house in the compound and all their needs, including meals, be taken care of by the rest of the extended household. This puzzles me. If multiple wives and thereby multiple widows all have to retreat to the mourning house, who does all the work, all the cooking and especially the work in the fields? And how did black mourning clothes come to be part of the ritual anyway when they plainly are not part of Swazi traditional dress? Perhaps they came with the missionaries in Victorian times and never went away?

Since mourning house seclusion in the kraal meant moving out of their own traditional huts, it would seem logical that they be taken over by others rather than stand empty. However, what may have worked in those traditional circumstances is not appropriate in urban settings or viable in modern nuclear families where the choice is between traditional mourning or surviving. Nowadays, like Eliza, the widow's earnings are often crucial for keeping the family together and two years of mourning are totally impractical with the extended family not around. Only 18% of Swazi women are in official polygamous households, but that doesn't seem to stop these unsuitable Swazi Laws and Customs being applied with a lot of pressure to the rest of the population, even those married under common law. This includes, quite often, property grabbing and eviction which has no logic in those different circumstances, only avarice. "Swazi culture" is a phrase too often used to cover sheer greed.

As Mswati 111 is Africa's last absolute monarch and the interpreter of what constitutes unwritten Swazi Law and Custom, he has it in his power to do something about this. In fact, in 1998 on his 30th birthday and the 30th anniversary of Independence, as a present to his people, he did decree that all widows could cast aside their mourning clothes and come out of seclusion especially to celebrate the event. Unfortunately, he did not also give them a present of the right to inherit, or access to land to grow some food, or permission to trade to help them out of poverty.

He could have used his prerogative in the case of Mzikayise Ntshangase's two widows who spent more than 5 years in the compound mourning house unable to leave or cook for themselves because there was some dispute about where their late husband was entitled to be buried, a vital part of Swazi ancestral tradition and until that was resolved, they had to stay where they were. He could have, but he didn't. In fact, the king inaugurated the dispute in the first place by refusing him the right to be buried with his ancestors due to some unresolved dispute whose origin no one seemed able to remember. Meanwhile the corpse was decomposing in the undertakers who complained bitterly that it was bad for business!

Although Swaziland, ie the King has signed countless international treaties on Human Rights granting equality to the sexes, recognising the rights of women etc, rather like the enthusiastic purchase of mementoes on holiday, on arriving home they're put into a drawer and left to gather dust, never seen again and certainly not acted upon. If anything, things have got worse instead of better. Even the 2005 Swazi Constitution granting the surviving spouse "reasonable provision" must be mouldering in someone's drawer in Parliament since nothing has been done to implement it in the ten years since its signing.

Luckily my colleague Eliza avoided becoming her brother-in-law's junior wife since he had a Christian and not a polygamous marriage and she was allowed to work and care for her children but she couldn't avoid the pressure of some of the other Swazi customs such as being dressed in full mourning for two years and various other taboos. As a visible manifestation of bad luck, superstitious people avoided her and there were occasions when bus drivers refused to let her board the bus. At the time when she joined us, more than a year after the fatal car accident, she had not yet received any insurance money but whether that was due to the custom of it reverting to the husband's relations, I can't say.

Jane Motsa, my first counterpart in the Education Department, had royal credentials and was engaged to, and eventually married her university lecturer fiancé. Sometime during our tea break scandalmongering I was told a young relative of hers was once forcibly escorted from her school by members of the King's bodyguard to be another of the King's many wives, but found when she got to the palace, she had just been preceded by another young teenager who had also been "escorted" there so, luckily, she could go back to school and avoid a life of luxurious boredom. Whether that is apocryphal or not, the case of Zena Mahlangu is certainly true and caused a furore between the royal house and the Judiciary when her widowed mother had the temerity to sue the royal guards who had kidnapped her 18 year old daughter from school. The King himself could, of course, not be touched as he was above the law. Since the judges upheld the mother's right to sue despite the royal household's order to drop the case, it eventually escalated to a schism between the independent judiciary and the King in which the rule of law lost out. The judges were sacked and the King appointed his own chief justice to carry out his orders. An unfortunate choice as it turned out.

My last counterpart as Head of Department was Ruby Dlamini. Unusually for a Swazi woman, Ruby was tall, approaching forty (if her grey hair was anything to go by), unmarried and had no children. I'm not sure who applied some pressure to change this situation but the partner they arranged for her to marry was surprising, to me anyway. The prospective bridegroom was a widower whose wife and children had been killed by lightning striking their homestead so now he was wanting a replacement or even replacements. Being a dutiful and obedient Swazi daughter, Ruby reluctantly went through with the marriage, but found excuses to remain at college during the week-ends instead of spending time up north with her new husband. Complaints trickled down and she was summoned to the Principal's office, given a lecture on wifely duties by Vilakazi and ordered to go home at weekends in the future. I think one of the best years of her life must have been her scholarship year at Newcastle University where she couldn't be got at. At least that was the impression I got when she came to visit me in England though, like most Swazi women, she bore her burdens stoically and in silence.

The male lecturers, with the exception of the Dreaded Dlamini, treated both their female colleagues and their own families with respect and consideration. Herbert Manzini was the first Deputy Principal. I think he might have been Zulu not Swazi and tried to bring some discipline and modern ideas into college life. Determined to enforce punctuality among a reluctant student body more attuned to the sun in the sky than the clock on the wall, he finally resorted to patrolling the corridors after breakfast with his Alsation. That got them getting to classes on time.

Apart from friends at the campus, club and Casino, I was on nodding and chatting acquaintance with a fair number of people in town like the garage hands, shop keepers, bank clerks and so on but the best glimpse of struggling Swazi women came from Harriet, my home help. As soon as word got around that Noma, my help, had tragically died, I had a stampede of poor, unemployed young women knocking on my door asking for employment. Really, once I had moved into a slightly bigger house and had managed to acquire a washing machine, I didn't need any more help in the house but the plight of the unemployed meant you just had to give someone a helping hand so Harriet came into my life. She was neat, intelligent, spoke fluent English and found dust in places I had never bothered to investigate.. She came walking up my path with a smiley little two year old toddling by her side and obviously needed a job pretty desperately. Her first partner had left her and their four children and her second had done the same once she'd had the little boy. I never discovered why these men just abandoned her and their children and I don't think she did either. They just left.

More than 50% of Swazi children are born illegitimate by our Western definition of that term but that doesn't allow for the complicated marriage and paternity rules of Swazi Law and Custom. Suffice it to say, even those have broken down from the rigid discipline days of the age regiments and the authority of the elders. Abandoned women and children are on the increase at an alarming rate. Harriet did what most Swazi women do in that predicament. They take their children back to the village homestead to Granny and look for a job. So her four older children joined her sister's five under Granny's care but so far she had still managed to keep the youngest with her.

Once, in general conversation when I remarked I would have to see Dr Lapping about something she got quite agitated and said she was very angry with him because he'd fitted her with a contraceptive coil and it hadn't worked and she'd got pregnant anyway. That rocked me back on my heels! It was the first time I'd heard of a Swazi woman doing that. On another occasion when I casually handed her a cup of tea she told me about the time she worked as a maid over the border in the Republic and had to drink her tea out of an empty baked bean tin because the madam wouldn't let her use a cup. All in all we believed Harriet deserved better than a part time cleaning job and eventually managed to get her a post as a shop assistant in the village much better suited to her obvious abilities, but alas, as a consequence, the smiley little boy had to join his many siblings and relations at Granny's homestead. The choices women have to make are never easy.

Sharing the Nation's Wealth

I look back now with a certain nostalgia to those days in the eighties when the burglars of Nhlangano behaved like gentlemen; when the man you knew had stolen your car tools had the decency to help push your car or even lend the odd spanner back to you; when the burglar who'd emptied your fridge and drunk all the booze, thoughtfully washed up and left your kitchen as tidy as he'd found it apart from the small matter of the eggs he'd boiled in the kettle ready to take away with the rest of the loot and then forgotten about. All of which happened to us, of course. In those gentler pre AK47 days, broadly speaking, you knew whom you were dealing with. It stood to reason, thieves who stole your food and your clothes but left your TV and hi fi had no use for electrical items, had, in fact, no power in their huts; small fry, redistributing a little of the nation's wealth.

I never lost quite enough to justify filling in the reams of forms necessary to claim from the insurance company so I let the premiums lapse. A fatal mistake since the next thing to go was son David's bike. We had brought it over from England and it was very distinctive, so much so that it was seen several times in the neighbourhood, or so people told us. We gave all the particulars to the local policeman and told him he was needed at the trap we had set. What we didn't realise then was that the culprit was the policeman's

122

brother. Inevitably, the trap failed and the bike was never seen again. We should have done what another neighbour did when he lost his garden furniture. He inspected the gardens in the neighbourhood and stole it back.

In the 80s, apart from the odd car theft, the nearest Nhlangano got to a major crime was the case of the amateur highwaymen. The van delivering the takings of the Supermarket to the bank was held up by two men at the crossroads and relieved of its load. That same evening an unlikely looking gambler appeared among the sophisticates at the roulette tables of the casino. Whenever he laid a new bet, he would bend down under the table, delve into a grey canvas bag and count out a fistful of change for his chips. It might as well have been labelled 'swag' and the management lost no time in calling in the police. Not known for their delicacy of touch, they stormed into the hotel, revolvers drawn, ready to shoot up the gaming tables and any one else who might get in their way. Only a swift offer of the freedom of the bar averted a nasty scene. Without a murmur of protest, the three policemen were persuaded to wait till the culprit left the premises to arrest him. I suspect this also had something to do with the profit motive of the casino since whatever was spent from the bowels of the Barclays bag belonged legally to the casino and could not be reclaimed. So when the bag was good and empty, which happened soon enough, the policemen were tipped the wink and jumped on their victim in the car park.

He must have sung like a canary, as the saying goes, because, next thing, our neighbour Harry was raided in the middle of the night and the rest of the money retrieved from his roof space. We had long suspected that he was the culprit who had stolen our car tools and the old shotgun that Robin had hidden in the top of the wardrobe. The gun dated back to his days on his farm and had put various wounded animals out of their misery and dispatched a few vicious black mambas who had taken a wrong turning into his farmhouse. Luckily the shotgun was empty though it was almost certainly used as the hold-up weapon. We didn't care to claim it back.

When the neighbour eventually came to trial, people like Doctor Lapping and the local sheriff spoke in his defense. His young wife had heart problems and needed medical treatment ... it wasn't easy being a coloured belonging neither to the Swazis or the Europeans. It cut no ice with the Magistrate who gave him five years in the local jail. However, six months into his sentence, when he was out with a working party clearing the golf course, he walked away when the guards weren't looking and was never seen again – not in Nhlangano anyway though plenty of his friends visited him in Soweto. There could of course be another explanation for this convenient blindness on the part of the guards but we won't go into that.

Mulling over the case in the club, the old hands were reminded of another case, the great bank robbery three decades or so back, up the hill at Hlatikulu. Hlatikulu had started life at the turn of the century as the southern outpost of the colonial administration because, in the absence of a proper road or any other form of swift communication, you could heliograph headquarters at Mbabane some hundred plus kilometres away – less as the crows or the light messages fly – from the top of the mountain. It was reported by the original surveyors to be the right spot to establish His Majesty's mandate since, being so high, "it was good for men and horses."... but darned hard on women, perhaps?

The little settlement eventually boasted a courthouse and jail, a hospital, a tin bungalow for the District Commissioner and of course, an Inn, the Assegai Arms, and a clubhouse. Once a week, overnight, Barclays Bank sent up two of its cashiers on horseback from over the border in Piet Retief to transact the payment \of wages and the banking of rents and taxes levied on the Swazi population. The thought of all this money left overnight proved too much for two of the local Boer characters, Jaap Potgieter, an itinerant sheep farmer and Fanjan

125

Jackson who worked for the Public Works Department. This was in the days before electricity arrived in this rural backwater, so there was no alarm device on the bank's lock-up ... and Fanjan did have access to all kinds of lovely public works items like bolt cutters ... and wheelbarrows.

Everything went to plan. The night was black and moonless. They had no problem getting into the lock-up and no problem loading up their wheelbarrow. But Fanjan, careless fellow, had picked a barrow sadly in need of a little oiling. The loud squeals as they trundled away the bags of money set the dogs barking and alerted the District Commissioner's guard who came to investigate, following the squeaking of the wheel in the blackness. On the challenge of "Who goes there?" Fanjan immediately took fright, yelling, "Don't shoot! Don't shoot! It's Fanjan Jackson," while Jaap Potgieter took to his heels and ran all the way down the mountain to Nhlangano, a considerable feat in total darkness. But like our neighbour, he got shopped by his partner in crime and went to jail.

I verified the truth of all this in the National Archives from back issues of the local paper and felt a certain sympathy for the two of them. But amusing though it all was, we felt it was time to put a stop to this violation of our home and the endless replacement of locks and broken windows. We decided to get a dog.

In the bungalow at the back of us lived an Afrikaner called Eckhart Ries who kept the local butcher's shop and bottle store. His frame matched his occupation; fat and florid with a huge beer belly which drooped over the tight waistline of his inadequate shorts. Despite his gruff manner and coarse language, he was quite a kindly man underneath, a fact he tried to keep hidden from the population in general --- just in case. In case of what I never quite worked out, but he certainly didn't want his tough image dented by rumours of a soft touch.

As soon as Eckhart heard us mention "dog" he insisted on making me a present of a little half grown Jack Russel terrier bitch, part of his litter of pups. We had really wanted a somewhat larger, fully-grown dog more likely to frighten off any burglar than one limited to savaging an intruder's big toe but it seemed boorish to refuse. Eckhart's dogs were his pride as was the little mixed race girl we saw playing in his garden. Eckhart wasn't her father. It wasn't generally known in the village, but that privilege belonged to a European teacher who had gone back home to England, abandoning mother and daughter. Eckhart took it upon himself to pick up the pieces, employ the mother as his cashier and house them both. For him to make the effort of polite conversation in English, a language with which he had difficulty, was privilege enough; to be the

127

recipient of one of his beloved dogs was an honour not to be refused so the little Jack Russel bitch entered our lives.

As a child I had been bitten by an enraged terrier so I had hopes that at least she might prove pugnacious, in spite of her size. To get her in the right aggressive frame of mind we named her Winnie, after that fearsome lady of anti apartheid fame. More Whiney than Winnie as it turned out. Whenever anyone approached her she would immediately lie on her back with her tail between her legs and make little whining noises of submission. I'd put her back on her feet and lecture her as one female to another about asserting herself, about her duties of guarding and standing on her own four paws. I'd make snarling and barking noises and pretend to attack in the hope of arousing some aggression. To no avail. She'd lick my face and roll over begging to be tickled. Servile and abject she was and servile and abject she'd remain and being Eckhart's generous gift, we were stuck with her.

Not so. Fate took a hand, a dramatic and final one. Eckhart came home one lunch time as usual, retired for his nap, as usual, and never woke up. His wife, who had "got religion" as he once confessed to us and from whom he had been parted for many years, arrived immediately from South Africa with his two grown up sons, put the mother and her little daughter out of the house and arranged for the funeral to be held over the border in Piet Retief, a dorp about as right wing as they come. Eckhart's Swazi customers and friends were very upset. With funerals being such a vital part of Swazi culture and since Eckhart had been an important figure in the village for so many years, it was felt essential for them to give him their support on his way to his ancestors. So they hired some transport and those who had the necessary papers to get across the border in the first place, set off for the church in Piet Retief. It took a lot of effort and expense. When they got there, they were told to stand outside the door, not because the church was full but because they were the wrong colour. The wrong kind of Christians.

Winnie got a new home, a mate and a litter of puppies who bullied her unmercifully and we set out to find ourselves "a proper dog". Little did we know.

It's a Dog's Life

We drove to the Dogs' Home in Mbabane. Dogs of all shapes and sizes and colours hurled themselves at us, yapping, tails wagging, begging us to take them home. In a large enclosure of his own, looking bored and superior lay what looked like a lion without his mane; a mixed breed Mastiff, Golden Labrador – mainly Mastiff judging by his huge head.

"Do take this one," urged the Swazi attendant "He's a lovely dog. From a very good home," he added as I made to turn away mentally calculating the cost of feeding such a large creature. Robin read the name on the gate, "Barnabus Berrange. Berrange? Is that the name of his previous owner?"

The attendant nodded.

"I know that name. Berrange. He was one of the lawyers at the Rivonia trials." said Robin excitedly.

That meant nothing to me.

"The Rivonia trials," he repeated, "When Nelson Mandela and those others were tried for treason. After they were convicted, it was too dangerous for Berrange to stay in South Africa so he came into exile in Swaziland."

Faint memories stirred, "And isn't he the one they tried to assassinate?"

Robin shrugged. Assassinations were a frequent

occurrence in Swaziland as the South African

Security Forces stormed over the border illegally and picked off whosoever they had a mind to. I looked into the cage with renewed interest.

"The old man, he just died," said the attendant.

"We'll take him," said Robin decisively and indeed, after the collective shame of the Piet Retief funeral episode, Barnabus seemed to have the perfect credentials. Then, just to show us that he wasn't one to be overwhelmed with gratitude like those other inferior dogs yapping away, and that we were on trial as much as he, he was car sick all the way home.

Once he recovered from the journey and settled in, he was lively and well behaved as far as we were concerned, anyway. He liked rough games and got quite excited but never hurt us in spite of his size. However, there were certain problems. One look at him was enough to terrify most Swazis and we discovered all too quickly that Barney was going to prove a huge embarrassment as the biggest racist in town. Neither of us believed in chaining a dog so no Swazi friend or neighbour, no student, workman or even regular employee could come to the house without Barnabus setting up a ferocious hullabaloo, snarling and barking from his side of the fence, racing the length of the garden throwing up the turf in a frenzy to get out and sink his teeth into something or someone as the unfortunate caller took fright, often screaming in terror as they ran. Serious callers stood their ground at the gate until the dog was safely shut up out of the way.

Even Ernest, the gardener, who actually liked the dog in spite of everything, would ask sadly, "Why does this dog hate me?" and to spare his feelings I tried to invent some plausible psychological canine history.

"It's nothing personal, Ernest," I reassured him, "It must be all gardeners. Perhaps he was kicked by one when he was a small puppy? They don't forget, you know. Or perhaps someone beat him with a spade," I added since the sight of one in Ernest's hands could always be guaranteed to set off a paroxysm of almost uncontrollable fury. Seemingly mollified, Ernest shook his head sadly and muttered to himself about the foolishness of some Swazis in the matter of dogs.

I began to half believe this nonsense myself but couldn't reconcile a dog owned by such a champion of non-whites, one who had risked his life and made himself a target, acting the way that Barnabus did. It didn't seem to add up. In an effort to lessen his aggression, we had him neutered. In consequence, he developed a resolute aversion to the vet, understandable under the circumstances, but murder whenever he was required to go for a rabies injection or developed tick fever or some other ailment. First he would try to hide his bulk under a bed or behind a bush and then he had to be manhandled by the two of us into and out of the car during the course of which, he always seemed have acquired a few extra heads and legs which were out when they should be in etc. Since we took care never to mention the dreaded V word in his hearing, how he knew the destination we had in mind remains a mystery.

Another of our bright ideas was to get him a companion so we got a collie bitch. Or rather, she got us by pushing her head into my lap and gazing at me so pleadingly she melted all my resistance. We hoped that by providing some company, some distraction, she might soften Barney's desire to kill every passer-by. For him, this was adding insult to his masculine injury. Being indifferent to her charms, she had little impact on his life but a great deal on ours.

Millie never stopped fussing or overwhelming us with boundless affection. Whatever we were doing, eating, reading, watching a video or even sleeping, a wet nose nuzzled up. Once rescued, this restless, excitable little collie was, perhaps, afraid of losing us and tried never to let us out of her sight. If we locked her up, she barked incessantly hour after hour so that was a non-starter. Since she could jump the gate with ease and made a nuisance of herself by barking and scratching on the door wherever we were visiting, we had to find strategies to persuade her to go home and wait for us. She soon learnt that if we walked off in the direction of town, or if we took the car, there wasn't much use following. So if we wanted to call on neighbours two doors away, we either had to get in the car, drive through the college gates and then double back or we had to set off in the opposite direction, walk around the campus until she'd given up and gone home to sulk and then sneak quietly up to their door. The crunch came one dark night when Robin was taking this circuitous route, creeping round the back of the college to call at the Oldridge household only two doors down from us and passed a friend, a European, whose wife was away on a visit, creeping round the other way to keep a tryst with a certain colleague of mine, a very curvaceous black lady he'd met at the club. The shock of being discovered immediately gave way to relief as Bill assumed that Robin was on a similar mission, a mission that had to be kept secret from the missus at all costs, nudge, nudge. Hiding from a dog? A likely story! Millie had to go. A Swazi vet's family with lots of children proved the ideal solution.

Reviewing the position, it began to occur to me that maybe I was doing Barnabus an injustice. Was he perhaps guarding me, as he had guarded Berrange? When we took him out for his daily run in the forest, he always positioned himself between us, slightly in front, when I took him alone, he kept to my side until

134

I told him to run free. That caused the most trouble. Even in the most isolated places, it was rare not to come across someone wending their way to some forest homestead, carrying water, delivering a message. Never just out walking. And anyone approaching, no matter how distant, was barked a warning before Barnabus chased them away. And of course, the more they screamed and ran, the more he chased. Pleas on my part to whoever it was to stand still usually fell on deaf ears, unsurprising given the size of the creature, which started the inevitable merry-go-round of dog chasing man and me chasing dog, yelling unheeded commands to heel.

Whenever someone did have the courage to stand still, Barnabus braked in full gallop, skidded to a halt, circled them suspiciously and awaited developments. Since I wasn't a political exile and didn't appreciate his efforts to guard my person from just about everyone, the developments usually consisted of him being dragged away by his collar, half choking and growling at the unfairness of it all. After all, we hadn't been burgled since he was around, I'll say that for him. On the other hand, every time we were away for any length of time we got a dog sitter so the house was never actually left empty.

At Christmas the campus was full of visiting children so we were anxious to avoid any incidents. Other dogs barking sometimes set Barnabus off and late Christmas Eve was just such an occasion. He barked and barked. Guilt about keeping the neighbour's children awake made us finally drag Barney inside and lock him in the kitchen with dire warnings to shut up. The following morning, because Robin's car was blocking mine, I borrowed it for an urgent errand in town.

"I thought you said you'd filled up with petrol," I said crossly when I got back, "The gauge was on empty. I almost didn't make it. How are we going to get out to your brother's for Christmas lunch with all the garages shut?"

"But I did fill up... at least, I think I did." said Robin, unsure now since he was notoriously absent minded. "Anyway, there's a spare can in the porch. We can use that."

Charming. Christmas day, my best outfit and I have to stand and hold a smelly funnel. Robin poured. Petrol gushed all over my feet.

"Oy! Look what you're doing!"

Robin poured the petrol more slowly. Still it poured into my best shoes. We looked at each other and simultaneously bobbed down to look under the car. Someone had cut the pipe and stolen the petrol!

"That's what happens when you leave your car standing on the road!" was all I could find to say,

136

"Don't say I didn't warn you. We'll have to take mine."

At least that still had some petrol. It also had a big hole where the radio cassette used to be!

Barnabus looked at us with a pained expression, put his head on his paws and closed his eyes to shut out this painful scene.

"I tried to tell you but you wouldn't listen! Stupid humans.

Let nothing you dismay

Christmas in the southern hemisphere in the middle of summer always seemed peculiar to me, especially since the trappings of the northern winter festival were rigorously adhered to by much of the population. It was probably due to the strong missionary influence, though the same couldn't be said for all the hotels milking the situation. There, Father Christmas made his entrance sweltering in his red robes with the sweat trickling from beneath his red hood, down the equally red expanse of his forehead to gather in globules at the promontory of his nose and drip into the cotton wool of his long beard if you were lucky, or onto the heads of the little children sitting on his lap reciting their wants if you weren't. Turkeys and flaming Christmas puddings were served while Jingle Bells rotated endlessly on the taped Muzak.

Since I hated it all, I often wondered subsequently why I opted to spend the Christmas of '84 at the new Piggs Peak Hotel and Casino in the mountains in the north of the country. It was partly, I suppose, to get away from the campus for a change, partly because, having a birthday on Christmas Eve, I wanted to be pampered for once instead of spending it in the usual fashion, slaving away for the following day's jollifications, as though they ever were – jolly, I mean. David was home from Waterford, and I also

138

had my friend Hilda visiting from Botswana, but the deciding factor, apart from the very good special introductory price offer, was the mastermind of their kitchens, Andreas Mankowitz, the German chef.

Andreas had been the chef at the hotel in Nhlangano when I first arrived. His creamy stroganoffs, crispy rostis, perfumed strudels promising cloves and cinnamon, almonds, apples and sultanas and succulent steaks were done to perfection. Dark and smoky outside with pink juices oozing from the tender flesh ones knife cuts through like butter. The memory of them makes my mouth water even now. A genius like that, one must forgive a volatile temper, forgive his demolition of the English language and his prima donna ways, forgive everything – well, almost – and focus on how lucky one was to have such a culinary wizard in a remote frontier outpost like Nhlangano.

Unfortunately his shapely, blonde young wife was not of the same opinion and took herself a lover; a slim young Austrian croupier with the unfortunate name of Ferie, pronounced as at the bottom of the garden. I suppose in African chauvinist terms, it was deemed not only normal, but desirable that Andreas should collect a mistress or two, but that extra-marital privilege did not extend to his wife. When Andreas found out what was happening, he beat Ferie up, leaving him a bit of a mess. There it would have ended for an African, honour satisfied, except he would probably have beaten up his wife too for good measure. Andreas didn't go that far, but Klaudia reported him to the authorities all the same. She identified him as a man wanted by the police in Germany for jumping bail while awaiting trial on a charge of manslaughter. Completely thrown by this unheard of treachery against the breadwinner of the family, the Swazi police nevertheless had no option but to inform the German Embassy and were instructed to lock Andreas up to await the arrival of an escort of German police to take him back.

The manslaughter charge, explained one of the police officers visiting the casino later, was the result of a fatal motor accident and not a crime passionel as village rumour suggested. The Swazi policeman enquired plaintively if nothing could be done to help this poor white man languishing in jail in Mbabane while the paper work got sorted out? Short of giving him the run of the jail kitchens and something other than the prisoners' daily meal of maize and beans to cook, there was nothing much that anyone could do. After visiting him in prison a couple of times, Robin could quite understand why the Swazi prison staff felt so sorry for him. He had languished in his little cell and lost a considerable amount of weight. But the run of the jail kitchen was exactly what they gave him in Germany when Andreas eventually got sentenced to eighteen months. And his German Prison Governor made sure he had the services of this top class chef all to himself. Lucky man!

The memory of Andreas and his exploits soon faded except on those increasingly rare occasions when we wanted a good celebratory meal. Since the casino had been the only decent place in town to eat, the lowering of standards was particularly marked and Andreas' departure was remembered with a certain regret. But life went on and eventually we went on leave overseas and made arrangements with a friend to collect us from the airport at Matsapha on our return.

But it wasn't the friend who was there to greet us. It was Andreas, irrepressible as ever. He had taken charge to surprise us with his reappearance. Since he had also combined this with re provisioning the hotel, we travelled the ninety kilometres home in a van with hundreds of pink and pimply frozen chickens as fellow passengers. Thousands of sausages and the welcome odour of mangoes and pineapples held the promise of feasts to come. But, ever restless, Andreas vanished again shortly after and resurfaced at the new hotel in Piggs Peak where we had run him to ground.

Piggs Peak, I was told, had nothing to do with four legged grunters. A prospector called Samuel Pigg had travelled over the mountains of the Highveld from the gold fields of Barberton and Pilgrim's Rest and actually found gold when panning the beautiful Popinyane river. Before the subsequent gold rush started in earnest, he registered his concession. Luckily for us, his name lasted longer than the gold and the mountains returned to their breathtaking beauty with man made forests the only concession to prizing wealth from the land. Much of the area has become national parkland, set aside in the teeth of desperate population pressure, in the hope of gaining a thriving tourist industry. I suppose that's why they also established the country's third hotel casino up there though the two types of tourist, the lover of the wild and the lover of constantly jingling slot machines are hardly compatible.

A huge area of the forest had been cleared and hillsides cut to make room for the new complex. They still lay raw and bare. The design and building contract had been given to the British firm of Tate and Lyle, which astounded me since I had only ever associated them with sugar. The hotel was unusual since, due to sanctions, every item in it, barring the building stones, had been imported from the UK. The reception area was panelled with beautiful close grained beech as were the fittings and furniture. A small atrium containing tropical plants and a couple of seats was a feature of the hallway. The elegant dining room with thick pile woollen carpets, upholstered dining chairs and matching curtains led straight out onto a terrace which rewarded one with the most beautiful views of the surrounding mountains. Even the china, cutlery and glassware were British. It was like suddenly being transported to another continent, especially in the bar where the barman had to hire you the one and only British old twenty pence piece, a florin in fact, to put in the slot to release the balls for the pool table. At the end of the game you had to take care to hand it back – or no pool, ever again! It was totally bizarre! Without converters which hadn't arrived yet, the guests were unable to use any electrical equipment they had brought with them because the power points and plugs were square pin and incompatible with the local and, needless to say, that included the televisions.

Andreas greeted us warmly and affably until we made the mistake of asking, "How are things?" So he told us, volubly giving vent to his frustration, hands waving, every other word starting with the same sound as sugar, as only the Germans know how. The plumbing, the kitchen equipment, dishwashers, cookers, mixers, shredders, the whole lot was imported from the UK without the necessary books of instructions on how to use them. Whenever anything went wrong or needed replacing, orders had to go back to England for the parts. It was a nightmare scenario, but it was nevertheless, a beautiful hotel in a beautiful setting.

"Although fairly high," went the guide book, "it is seldom really cold here. Rain falls mainly in the summer months between October and March and is mostly fairly soft and misty, lending to the forest regions an atmosphere which is reminiscent of Europe. The moist, earthy, leafy fragrance intensifies this characteristic."

Possibly the architects had read the same guide when they designed the hotel but the local God of weather certainly had not. At about half past three the sky began to darken and became so black we had to turn on the lights. As the clouds got closer and closer, a ferocious wind got up picking up anything loose left lying around – and there was plenty of that on the unfinished site – and tossing it into the air. Great flashes of lightning lit up the forests again and again followed almost immediately by deafening thunder. The flashes ricocheted from mountain to mountain and then one of the pylons exploded among the trees in a spectacular display, sending giant, crackling firework displays sizzling into the air as everything went black. All through the forest there were sounds of crashing trees and then the rain came, not soft and misty but lashing down in seemingly solid sheets driven horizontally by the force of this terrific wind, crashing on the windows. People began to panic,

144

moving away from any glass and seeking the company of others, groping in the dark. Staff ran around giving out candles (which often blew out) and then were preoccupied scurrying to and fro with buckets and mops moving furniture and rescuing glassware. The woman who kept the little stable of horses became hysterical about their fate, as well she might, when their wooden shelter went flying through the air past the windows. With a loud scream she rushed out into the storm determined to save them. At first we huddled in the inner candle-lit sanctum of the bar drinking out of fear but after a couple of hours, although it was still raining hard, the storm had abated somewhat, the sky got a little lighter and we ventured out to see what was happening. What a scene! In the foyer the atrium was rapidly filling with water, already above the level of the tropical plants which were waving like weeds in a giant goldfish bowl. The tiny drain in the middle might have been adequate for rain that was "soft and misty" but hopeless for the tropical downpour we were experiencing. Staff rushed around the dining room carrying out chairs and tables to roll up the sodden woolen pile carpet while others fetched ladders to remove the curtains. Since the terrace was at the same level as the dining room and the water had nowhere else to go. It had poured into the room at a tremendous rate, ruining the place before it was even properly open. Outside, the red-brown earth of the bare hillside had been washed down into the swimming pool turning it into chocolate sauce, while some had taken another route into the front entrance like a lava flow

With no power, there was no means of drying anything. With no power but a small emergency generator, Andreas pointed out, there was no way of keeping all the Christmas food fresh. Added to which, since gambling was now also impossible, many of the guests got into their cars as soon as they were able and headed back to the Republic and the certainty of ESCOM power and safe water. So, aided and abetted by Andreas, we spent Christmas by candlelight eating our way through a mountain of luxurious food we could never normally have afforded like lobsters and oysters, salmon and smoked trout, to name but a few. The turkey we rejected in favour of the more exotic. David, at sixteen, had no mean appetite but even he called a halt after lobster number four.

On Christmas day, still without power, we went for a long walk in the forest and beside the river. Everywhere there was evidence of destruction, but it was a swathe of destruction. The first two rows of trees were unmarked, the next six rows were sliced in half, mile after mile, as though a giant sword had chopped through them. It was quite extraordinary.

On Boxing Day we staggered home pounds heavier still wondering why on earth anyone would want to go to the expense of shipping an entire hotel out from England – and building it as though it was located in a Surrey countryside. We came to the conclusion Tate and Lyle might do better confining their activities to marketing sugar. Someone else must have agreed with us because it was firebombed shortly after. Actually religious zealots were suspected because after it was bought by another company and rebuilt much more cheaply with South African materials, it was burnt down for a second time. We never returned. After all, Andreas had left after the first bombing disappearing somewhere into the hinterland of Bophuthatswana so there was no feast to look forward to, but we did plan a trip to Sun City. After all, you never know…

The Pigg's Peak hotel pool 2016

Dreams and nightmares

Willi Lotte had a dream. Most whites in Swaziland did. They dreamt of making a quick fortune, of taming the bush and covering the hills with high yielding crops, of being the lords of their manor, bringing enlightenment to the Swazis – which meant the Western and therefore the "right" way to do things – especially the missionaries. Willi's dream was to build a Portuguese mansion. And so he did. With its two stories of round rooms and horned towers, round balconies, round stairs and round furniture, it was utterly hideous and Willi loved it. Still, it was a talking point and the folks around the club bar loved to talk, or rather, to scandal.

Willi loved his house all right, they said. In fact, he was so obsessed with it, his wife left him, it swallowed his money leaving him bankrupt and rumour had it he'd been arrested for murder. At least, it wasn't just a rumour, but what wasn't clear was who exactly he was supposed to have murdered and why. After all these years no one seemed entirely sure, though some thought it should have been his wife and wasn't. Consensus had it, it was someone in a drunken brawl.

"He's in prison then?" I wanted to know.

"There is no prison for murder, only hanging."

"But he never hung, did he?" someone butted in,"Old

149

Doctor Lapping and that lawyer Auguste Language, between them, they got him off. What's that they say in the courts?"

"... of unsound mind?" suggested the barman.

"Yes, that was it. Old Lapping had him certified to save him from the hangman. Said he'd had a nervous breakdown, or something. Mad I call it. Well he had to be, didn't he?"

I thought of the Portuguese mansion in the middle of the no nonsense four-square-walls-and-a-tin-roof architecture of the rest of the village and was inclined to agree.

Then there was Victor Leibrandt. He had a dream of playing the big white chief. With several Swazi wives, an assortment of offspring and a position of some importance among the King's Ministers, he was well on the way to realising his ambition. Notwithstanding all that, he was still terrified of some Swazi attack; so terrified that he fortified his farmhouse with high walls, a watchtower and impregnable underground rooms where he could lock himself away. As soon as his mentor, the old king died, his dream turned into a nightmare. He feared the worst, announced a mysterious illness, left the country "for treatment" and returned only a couple of years later when the dust of the changeover had settled.

Not that he didn't have some cause for concern. Despite almost a hundred and fifty years of missionary activity with the blessing of the various kings, there were some Swazi practices which persisted – rarely, it's true, and usually secretly – and one of them was ritual murder. There was a belief, reinforced by a few of the witch doctors, that certain body parts had magic properties to bring strength or good fortune or to neutralise an evil spell. Perhaps because he himself had embraced the African custom of polygamy and was more closely associated than most whites with Swazi customs and beliefs through his various wives, Leibrandt knew a thing or two about ritual murder.

Another case involved Mitchell, an American sea

Captain who had bought a farm only a few miles up the hill from Nhlangano towards Hlatikulu and whenever his ship docked at Durban, he spent his leave developing his land ready for his retirement: his dream farm. He loved riding around on his tractor levelling the land ready for crops. This proved his undoing when the heavy steel bar he was dragging along behind the machine to smooth the top soil, caught in a steep bank and jackknifed with the tractor which fell on top of the Captain, killing him instantly. They buried him on his beloved farm. His widow was left with only a small pension, the undeveloped farm and a huge problem. There was hardly any water. After exploring most avenues, she called in the local sangoma much as we might employ the services of a water diviner. When his job was successfully completed and it came to settling up, the sangoma was quite willing, he said, to accept cash or perhaps payment in kind of some sort. Since her cash was in short supply just then, he would even take a cheque but on no account would he touch American Express! Whatever form of payment he eventually accepted, it was discovered soon after, that the Captain's grave had been dug up and his head removed. It was never found again.

I don't suppose the Captain would have minded giving his widow a head start, so to speak though I very much doubt if the incident can be explained as a

152

part payment. Surely not? Nor do I think Leibrandt worried so much about losing his head when he was dead as when he was still alive although the usual trophies were more in the line of hearts, sexual organs, livers or particularly placentas. It's said the hospital mortuaries do a lucrative trade on the QT even now.

And it wasn't an exclusively Swazi affair. In the fifties, down at Big Bend, an eccentric old lady, a European called Mrs Hewitt who farmed all by herself, was found murdered and mutilated. Two other Europeans, a couple of shopkeepers called Von Wissel, suddenly found themselves under arrest on a charge of ritual murder. They languished in jail for over a year before they were exonerated and the charges dropped.

One very important Minister, let's call him Minister M., was not so lucky in 1978, which was hardly surprising, since human remains were found in his fridge. What was surprising was that anyone even dared to investigate him, certainly not the Swazis. It fell to a British Police officer on contract to Swaziland to do the necessary. Even then, he almost got away with it. Another man was arrested, charged with murder and faced the death penalty. From jail, he wrote Minister M. a letter demanding that he use his contacts to get the charges dropped or he would reveal Ms involvement in the matter. The letter landed on the Minister's desk and, naturally enough, his secretary opened it, read the contents – and fled. As soon as he saw the letter already opened, Minister M. realised the secret was out and departed for South Africa "for clinical treatment" or so the story went. It didn't help. The grisly contents of the refrigerator were evidence enough. So how did the story end?. Some said the Minister drank weed killer and died an excruciating death, some that no action was taken. I haven't been able to find evidence either way and the Swazi Police keep these things well hidden so there it has to be left..

Dreams of enlightenment weren't altogether failures though. Ritual murders were regarded by almost all the population with the horror they deserved. Sometimes communities, despairing of the police and the Department of Public Prosecution to get their act together, took matters into their own hands and chased the criminals from their area or even, as in Nsangwini, stoned them.

The missionaries have struggled hard to educate their flocks to the worth of human life. In fact, in the previous century Swaziland was so awash with various Missions all vying to educate the locals to their particular brand of Christianity, they were almost kidnapping pupils from each other. There must have been about twelve or so different missions on our little patch alone. The air of rivalry is still there though they each do sterling work in the fields of education and health.

The different kinds of Missions and missionaries and cults are intriguing especially the Church of Zion, a strange Christian sect which had, somewhat surprisingly, originated in Illinois in the US. and has no relationship to Jewish Zionism. Now it has assumed the Africanisation of European beliefs. There are lots of different splinter sects with an equal variation of beliefs, but all the preachers claim to have the power of healing and, without the regulations the inyangas employ, there is nothing to prevent them making those claims. The leaders of the red coat Jericho sect claim to turn water holy which they then bottle and send home with their followers, presumably at a price. With no regulatory body, many of the leaders are charismatic, powerful orators who claim to have seen visions or perform miracles and thereby get a following. There is nothing to stop them promoting themselves to be Bishops and Archbishops as far as I can see. Claims about seven headed monsters, of staying under water for several months and similar allegations made by the likes of Zionist Archbishop Mbonisi Shongwe are given credence by some of their followers. Most though, are more mainstream sects. Some dress up in long white robes with green sashes, some red and blue robes, some blue and white. The headgear varies from golden crowns to pith helmets and everything in between. They march along the road with their lances and banners singing what I presume to be hymns, with a distinctive African rhythm and every Easter there is a grand three day congregation when they all come together, a sea of colours and march before the king. The Zionists have a very substantial following which obviously fulfills a need and although they call themselves Christian, I see it more as a halfway house between Christianity and traditional African beliefs.

There was a bungalow in the Nhlangano known as the American Missionaries' house. Houses had a habit of keeping the designations of their original owners even after they had gone away. Their bungalow on the corner had the accoutrements of another, more sophisticated world. It had air-conditioning! – superfluous in this part of the country but that made it all the more noticeable. It was bigger than most of its neighbours, well protected with burglar bars, unusual in the eighties but not alas, any longer, and also boasted a spacious double garage for their two large station wagons. It could only have belonged to Americans. It still had an air of newness about it, understandable under the circumstances since the American Baptists had occupied it for less than a year before moving on.

It's intriguing to speculate what their expectations of

the place could have been. Were they disillusioned so soon or did duty call them elsewhere, although no one seemed to remember the reason for their rapid departure. I liked to imagine that they had moved north to Kenya, that they were, perhaps, the same American Baptist Missionaries my friend Ruth told me about. Based in Kericho, the lonely tea area in the middle of the country, the Americans had tried hard, she said, to convert the Kenyans to their particular brand of Christianity by improving their education and well-being at the same time. Given the circumstances, that invariably involved preaching the gospel of birth control. Granted, this was the pre-Aids era but right from the start, just like the Swazis, the men of Kericho vehemently rejected any interference with their sex life, many even believing it to be some plot of the white man to weaken the black. In Swaziland, at that time, the government had gone as far as closing down the birth control clinics the UN had set up by claiming that they were un-Swazi. Undaunted, the Baptist missionaries in Kenya then decided they might do better concentrating on the women. Since there wasn't enough money or medical expertise to fit them with coils or issue birth control pills, they distributed their stockpile of condoms instead with instructions to persuade their men to "place them on their organs." Either it was the American conviction that no one could learn anything unless it was fun, or to emphasize the fact that this was American Aid, the condoms were patterned with stars and stripes. It made no difference whatsoever to the birth rate but balloons sporting the star spangled banner cheered up many a celebration in the neighbourhood.

But to get back.

Dreams I had aplenty but what of nightmares? One such occurred when I was on teaching practice supervision at Mahamba primary school. I accidentally opened the door of an empty room to reveal a child being beaten with a switch slowly and deliberately by a woman teacher. The child received each blow in total silence, as, no doubt, she had been warned. Biting her lips in agony, silent tears streamed down her face. As outsiders, we college tutors were forbidden to interfere with the running of the schools but I longed to snatch the switch from the teacher's hand and give her a taste of the same or, better still, get her sacked. But that would never happen in Swaziland where beating is the norm, wives included. I must have stood there with such a shocked look on my face, the switch was lowered, the child sent back to her class and I closed the door with a muttered apology.

Three strokes of the cane were, and still are now in the 21st century, actually permitted by law but invariably exceeded. Corporal punishment is out of control, sometimes causing real injuries but the teachers are never prosecuted, so why not indulge in a bit of sadism? Should the punishment be so extreme it results in death, it has been known for just a fine of $27 to be levied and life to carry on as usual after that. Is that all the life of a child is worth? And all I could do then was close the door and make a mental note to have yet another session with my students about punishment.

You need to beat a child when it is stupid they told me. What gives you the idea, I'd ask them, that a pain in the behind or anywhere else will transfer to enlightenment between the ears? Not only is that not going to happen but it has the opposite effect. Think about it. If you're afraid of something you can't think straight. Fear of pain inhibits learning. So, let's look at the schools in Swaziland where beating is not allowed. There are some, mainly company or ex company schools. Do those children perform any worse because they are not beaten? The unanimous verdict of my students was always that they performed better. Right, quietly leaving aside the mainly middle class status of the pupils which would affect any result, that's one argument demolished.

In all my years of teaching, I told them, I have never hit a child. I don't think they believed me. Surely that was not possible. I confess I've been tempted once or twice on occasions of extreme stress but what would that have achieved? It would ruin the relationship between pupil and teacher and instead of being based on respect it would be based on fear. All that it proves is that I, the adult, am bigger and stronger than you. So what? If I beat up someone in the street I would be in trouble and charged with assault. If you, as my child's teacher, the person to whom I have entrusted their welfare and safety, beat him or her, then surely you are also guilty of assault. Are our helpless children not entitled to more protection than a stranger in the street? And if my child misbehaves, then I am the one who should sort it out.

But they all thought children should be beaten, as they were themselves. They had needed it, they said, to grow up as good, respectful people. They tried to outdo each other with examples of punishment meted out to them: holding a heavy stone over your head for God knows how long, squatting for hours as if sitting on air, digging a hole as deep as your height. The list went on. The children will be spoilt without corporal punishment. It was for their own good. Now where have I heard that before? Surely it's better to explain to children why they shouldn't do certain things, to reason with them so they understand why certain things are undesirable and monitor themselves? But in the end, losing patience, we just told them, as far as we in the Education Department are concerned, you are forbidden to beat any child on your teaching practice and if you do, there will be serious consequences. We'll show you other ways of dealing with a class of children. If I can do it, so can you.

Despite countless attempts over the decades by bodies like UNESCO, Save the Children, UNICEF, NGOs and Church organizations to get Swaziland to fall into line and stop beating children and although the Government signs every treaty intending to do just that, it has singularly failed to do so. In 2011 after the House of Assembly passed the Children's Protection and Welfare Bill and the Sexual Offences and Domestic Violence Bill, 495 cases known to have been reported to the police had no follow up or action taken. Between 2014-2015 over 1,000 cases of child sexual abuse were reported to the police with the same result. Nothing!

Between 2012 and 2016, over 4,500 cases of severe school beatings have taken place according to Save the Children and those are just the ones we know about. Not only are teachers beating children so hard, some with over 200 strokes of the cane, some causing unconsciousness and once even death, but there is "state sponsored torture of children" much of it carried out by the police. Although in the Children's Protection and Welfare Act which the government of Swaziland signed it defines abuse as "any form of harm or ill treatment deliberately

161

inflicted on a child", the constitution still supports "lawful and moderate chastisement for purposes of correction." This is supposed to allow just three whacks of a cane, but is totally ignored by the majority of teachers and more sadly, by the parents who tolerate and even condone this violence against their children in the name of education.

The Shirt Factory Do

We did try to warn them, we old Swazi hands, but they dismissed all our well meant advice. What did we country bumpkins understand about business – or politics? So they went ahead anyway, the new owners of the factory, issuing formal written invitations to the people they thought important in the Swazi community – which somehow included almost all the expatriates and whites in Nhlangano, including Robin and I. They also made sure those left out would stay out by building a huge fence round the factory compound to keep out the undesirables.

It was to be a really impressive function to celebrate, yet again, the opening of the ill-fated shirt factory – this time, in 1987, by efficient South African entrepreneurs. And this time to produce, not shirts but chipboard which seemed sensible, since the village was surrounded by some of the most extensive man-made forests in Africa.

It was the enterprising Taiwanese who had first built the shirt factory – the only factory in this rural backwater – to provide much needed employment in the area, not to mention cheap shirts. It was the South Africans who forced them to close down when they eventually got wind of it (fearing the undercutting of their own manufacture) by the simple expedient of slapping an extra tax of 30% on their imported raw

163

materials. Since Swaziland was a member of the Southern African Customs Union and South Africa its biggest, richest and strongest member, controlling all the ports as well, the Swazis had no option but to comply. But it rankled.

Then it was in turn a paint factory, until the owners blew the cash incentive provided by a grateful government and disappeared. It then became a furniture factory run by two one-eyed Irishmen, which the local wits dubbed Cyclops Enterprises. One fine night Patrick, and most of the valuable tools vanished and Terry got arrested by mistake by an over eager Swazi constable who couldn't believe his luck when he found a one-eyed Irishman propping up the bar at the local hotel, calm as you please; an easy mistake to make, as the Superintendent pointed out when they released him. Not only was it hard to credit that Nhlangano had not one, but two one-eyed Irishmen, but Europeans all looked alike to Africans anyway.

This time though, it was really going to take off. After all, South African business enterprise had taken charge. A huge quantity of machinery arrived from Belgium and was installed in the hollow shell and local labourers were taken on. Invitations for the grand opening were sent to local and national dignitaries, business executives and wives from SA, the press and TV. Biggest scoop of all, the young

King himself was coming. It was to take the form of a splendid sit down dinner and buffet. They even booked His Highness's favourite pop group, Hot Lips Mabuza and his Go Go girls.

The local hotel was honoured with the task of organising the food. They had never had such a huge order before, and were unlikely to have such a one again, so they really pulled out all the stops. The kitchens took on the semblance of a military campaign HQ. Extra provisions and cooks were summoned from all parts of the little kingdom and lorry loads of fresh fruit and vegetables ordered from Durban. And then it happened. Rumour has it the laden lorries were already on their way up when some elderly member of the royal household who could remember further back than most, decided it was the time of "the drying of the tears" and celebrations of any kind, during that period of mourning, were strictly taboo! The tears to be dried were those shed for the young king's father, King Sobhuza 11, who had died five years previously in 1982. Since he had reigned for over 60 years, it was no wonder such matters of protocol had become somewhat hazy. His body had been taken to the royal caves, south of Nhlangano, sitting bolt upright in a sedan chair, ready to spring to the defence of his nation, if needed, and now it was the duty of the young King to pay the corpse a visit. And no grand

165

opening until the period of mourning had passed.

This turn of events shook everyone, except perhaps those old enough to remember, way back, or more likely, to have heard tell of some other elaborate preparations made by the British Colonial Administration for the funeral on the death of the old, much respected, NdlovoKhasi, or Queen Regent, as the British preferred to call her, grandmother of the last king. Dignitaries had hastened to the kingdom from various corners of the empire, all dressed in their gold braided diplomatic finery with their white gloves and plumed hats, including a representative of King George V. When everyone was ready and assembled, they discovered the bird had flown or gone to earth, so to speak and there would be no state funeral as such. The Swazis had made their own arrangements and buried the old lady the day before with all due ceremony according to their own traditions, so that was that.

Anyway, to get back, several weeks later, the opening celebrations were all on again. Fresh banana trees, graceful draperies covering the machines, miles of streamers in national colours transformed the factory interior into a colourful arena. Long tables seating hundreds were exquisitely laid and decorated. An elaborate array of cutlery and glassware surrounded pretty individual helpings of hors d'oeuvres. The interior designer had excelled

166

herself over the decorations of fruit and loaves forming beautiful sculptured displays along the side tables. Equally elaborate arrangements had been made only to admit guests with an invitation card. To make sure, some of the local labourers were recruited as guards and bouncers. The local choir, sibhaca dancers and the factory workers were to be fed in the field outside the high perimeter fence. The planning was business like, security tight and nothing could go wrong, or so they said.

Free drink was liberally dispensed all around the grounds as soon as guests started to arrive: Boer businessmen in tight suits with frilly wives in high heels, government officers, some in Western clothes, some in the red, black and white cloth of Swazi national dress with pompoms across their shoulders and their wives in every sort of fashion but mostly carrying large handbags. Those on duty or outside the fence looked on with great envy. Eventually, all the guests were persuaded to take their seats inside.

It started well enough with the royal entourage on a special dais, except the King, of course, who still kept the tradition of eating privately with the royal taster to make sure he wasn't poisoned. One hopes he had dropped the other traditional precautions against witchcraft like the gathering of the royal hair and toenail clippings, etcetera – the etcetera presumably unnecessary now with the advent of modern plumbing.

As soon as the hors d'oeuvres placed in front of each guest were finished, or even before, the more enterprising of the Swazi women were milling around the buffet and piling everything from chicken legs, steaks, vol au vents, rice, salad, cream cakes and jelly onto the same plate. If nothing else would fit the pyramid, they opened their capacious handbags and swept in whatever they could hold. Those behind, finding the buffet denuded, looked around for more, found none and dismantled the sculptured decorations of icing, loaves, fruit and greenery. Waiters carrying trays of refills on their heads mysteriously found them empty by the time

168

they reached the buffet tables.

The uninitiated watched this performance in total disbelief.

"Did you see that? Everything's disappeared!" said a shocked guest sitting next to old Annie, the missionary.

"Well, what do you expect?" was her calm reply,, "If you don't invite everyone, the others expect their share to be brought back for them. Swazi custom is welcome one and all and this is Swaziland. Anyway, I did warn those South Africans not to have a help yourself buffet – but no. We know how to handle our Blacks, they said. Our Blacks! The arrogance! Serves them right."

Things calmed down a bit when first the King and then the pop group appeared. It was real sophisticated stuff from Soweto with a back up group of nubile young girls in beaded bras and very short skirts swinging their hips and gyrating at a fantastic tempo, so sinuous they could have been made of rubber. It was all too much for those outside. The guards and bouncers had watched their fellow citizens, their cousins and uncles downing free drink after free drink. They could smell the meat and hear the music, so when all the guests disappeared inside it was only natural that they should also have a celebratory drink – and then a few more. After that it

169

didn't seem to matter that the workers down the field had cut holes in the fences, that the schoolchildren were crowding in to catch a glimpse of their King and listen to the music.

When things were getting really lively and the old men's eyes were glazing over with fond memories as they watched the waggling hips and breasts of the Go Go girls, the Elders whisked the King away. The party broke up in a shambles and those guests who had declined the scrum had to go home to boil an egg or open a tin. To some it seemed an uncivilized rout, to others a triumph of native cunning over racial imperialism. Sadly, it didn't end like that.

It was finally revealed that the old shirt factory was actually being used as a front for tax and currency fraud. Invoices for the purchase of new machinery were presented while second hand throw-outs were installed and the money difference lodged in a Swiss bank account. No chipboard was produced and when the scam was discovered and the perpetrators put on trial, the factory gates were locked once more; the holes in the fence never repaired and the wind whistles its own music from the dais while the shirt factory awaits another Cyclops or Pygmalion to bring it back to life.

Which will not speak its name

No one at the College ever spoke to me about witchcraft. In fact, the subject was studiously avoided perhaps because all the staff or most of them, at least, had been educated in mission schools where the subject was strongly frowned upon and roundly condemned. Even when discussing handicapped children, who were often denied education and hidden away because they were believed to be cursed and might contaminate those around them, the subject was taboo. Yet one only had to go to the market to see the variety of "cures" love potions or muti to get you through your exams, to cure an illness or bad luck, to realise just how common these beliefs were. Once, to general indignation, someone even dug up the smooth turf of the soccer pitch in the national stadium to plant some muti by the goal to ensure victory for the home side. I'm not sure what was supposed to happen when they changed ends at half time and they lost anyway.

I had no trouble with inyangas, the herbalists, who were often consulted first before recourse to more expensive Western medicine. They had, after all, been plying their trade for centuries before Western medicine arrived and much of a pharmacist's stock comes from plants originally. Although, as one sees in any Swazi market, an inyanga's stock also includes animal substances. In addition, it requires

171

the use of certain ritual for any prescription to work effectively. They tend to take a holistic view to divine the problem, seek out mental or physical causes and apply the appropriate treatment. In order to weed out charlatans, the inyangas have developed courses, established the Swazi Traditional Healers Association and charge set fees. In keeping with the 21st century, many now even advertise their services on the internet! It might be worth mentioning at this point those Zionist preachers who also claim the power of healing but have no regulatory force behind them. The problem many Western trained doctors have is to reconcile modern medicine with traditional beliefs. The problem many inyangas have is to recognize those ailments that are beyond their scope and need western intervention. With over 8,000 practitioners (including Sangomas) and only 150 medical doctors in the whole of Swaziland, it is little wonder over 80% of the population uses them. Clearing up after the inyangas had 'had a go' with his patients used to drive Doctor Lapping mad, so he said, but then, lots of things did that.

The distinction between herbalism and divination has, perhaps, become somewhat blurred but, whereas anyone can choose and opt to take courses to become an inyanga, sangomas, it's said, are chosen by the ancestral spirits themselves as recipients of their healing powers and have no choice in the matter. The gift of healing has to be accepted and a two year apprenticeship undergone. Many of the practitioners are women easily recognizable by their fringed, red ochre hairstyles. They can receive and pass on the wishes of the ancestors in a number of ways, among them interpreting dreams, going into a trance, through dance and song, or, a favourite, interpreting the throwing of the bones. A sangoma's healing power is considered superior to both western medics and those of the inyangas because it comes from the ancestors who embody the essence of what it means to be Swazi. Despite many sangomas being women, the world of ancestors is exclusively patrilineal. Not only that, but they keep the status that they enjoyed in life. There is no levelling out by death. The more recently dead are more accessible for help because they are more familiar with the family and their needs, but they can be asked to contact the long dead who have progressed to higher planes.

Although the Swazi believe in God the creator, the Supreme Being who fashioned the earth, he is not worshipped nor has any sacrifices made to him. It is the ancestral spirits who influence everything that happens to you; your welfare, health, possessions, careers and family and the Sangoma who mediates between the two worlds. In many other cultures there are similar beliefs about the ancestors and their influence on our lives. Take the modern, highly industrialised, Japanese for example. However, both inyangas and sangomas condemn ritual murder and resent immediately being blamed whenever a new case comes up.

That leaves the witchdoctors, the practitioners of the black arts. I'm not sure of the special local name that exists for them. There must be one but none of my Swazi acquaintances cared or dared to utter it. If mentioned at all, they are known as witchdoctors. Hilda Kuper in "The Swazi" refers to 'batsakatsi' but right word or wrong, we are speaking of people widely regarded as being responsible for evil deeds and ritual murders. Actually that is a misnomer. As Themba Shongwe puts it in her research of the subject, some immoral, not to say evil superstitions still prevail but the outcome is murder pure and simple where "some body parts are taken for potions that it is believed, will make the recipient stronger and wealthier."

Neither, alas, is it a thing of the past. It is a dark and secret part of politics in Swaziland. Not so secret perhaps since even in 2003, according to the BBC news, when an election was due, the King himself said,

"During election times, we tend to lose our grandmothers, grandfathers and young children. They just disappear. But I want to warn you all that you should not resort to ritual murder to boost your

174

chances of election."

Since political parties are banned and the King appoints most of the positions, voting is for individual candidates with some put forward by the chiefs. Research has shown that leading up to and during elections every five years right up to 2018, at times of political insecurity, the known incidences of people disappearing, especially the vulnerable, and known ritual murders actually went up. The emphasis being on the word known. This implies that those seeking positions of power and patronage will use any means available to get there. In 2008 the government banned a national march against ritual killings although the King himself had publicly condemned them. The reason given by government ministers was that it would bring bad publicity to Swaziland. I'm not sure I understand the logic of that since the march would show positive public anger and revulsion against disgusting deeds. The suspicion is that it was too close to home. MPs and Ministers might have been implicated. The fact that hardly anyone is ever caught or convicted implies cover up and protection at the very top. One can't help concluding that had elections been more democratic with voting being on questions of policy rather than individual patronage, some children's lives might well have been saved.

Although the known killings are only supposed to

average eight to ten a year, there is the curious case of David Simelane who in 2004 after his arrest, admitted to 63 such killings, some dating back to 2001 and even took police to some of the remains and burial sites. Since he had no job, no money and no car, how was he able to lure his victims with promises of jobs and how did he transport the bodies to the remote forest locations where they were found? The Swazi police decided they needed the help of the South African Police, especially with DNA testing of the remains. After 5 years of building the case against Simelane, both senior investigators had died and left no paper work or records of the case behind. By 2011 five of the original eleven PCs had died, probably of AIDS and much of the evidence had disappeared. The SA police dropped out, complaining of lack of co-operation, and the suspicion was that he must have been part of a powerful syndicate. There were also allegations that someone had tried to poison him in jail. The implications of that are all too clear. He did come to trial a few years ago in 2011 and was found guilty in 2012. However, since only the King can actually order a hanging and by 2015 he had still not made up his mind, David Simelane is still languishing in jail with no decision as to his future – or lack of it.

These horrendous practices are found in other African countries too. Albino adults and children are particularly vulnerable. As the authorities in Burundi and Tanzania cracked down, the killers travelled further south. It is also big business as the parts can sell for anything up to $75,000 dollars. Partly this is due to the high incidence of HIV and AIDS, the desperation of the sufferers and the curious beliefs surrounding their cures which provide the killers with ready markets. It is also going through political and economic uncertainty which always affects criminal activity. But I think we can safely assume that the killings have more to do with greed than traditional beliefs. There is also a ready market for transplants in the more affluent countries of the world which have long waiting lists of patients and insufficient donors. This might also be a motivation, although this would imply a sophistication of transport operations which I doubt is available. People smuggling is also big business and rife in Swaziland at the moment with so many vulnerable orphans.

Trying to defend the indefensible, some Ministers (the guilty ones, perhaps) have pointed out that in the West doctors do sometimes remove organs from the brain dead, transplant hearts and kidneys, transfuse blood or graft skin. Hardly a valid comparison, the one being to save lives, the other to take lives of innocent victims. In Britain the days of Burke and Hare and their 16 victims are long gone and so are the experimental horrors of Germany's concentration camps. Since Mswati promises to bring Swaziland into the 21st century by 2022, here seems a good place to start. What is harder to achieve is a change of belief to a level which does not cause harm and that can only evolve organically. It wasn't all that long ago that Christians in the West believed in satan and hell and damnation and previous to that, in the sixteenth and seventeenth century belief in witchcraft was fairly common in the west and even America (think of the Salem witches).

There are still beliefs now that prayers to the saints can change your fortune; six million pilgrims a year go to places like Lourdes for miraculous healing; spiritualists allegedly can put you in touch with the departed; Buddhists believe in many reincarnations; fortune tellers or astrologists that they can foretell your future. The list goes on. Also, on a more modest level, there is a belief among some of the faithful, in the efficacy of some body parts to enhance good fortune. These are mainly, of course, body parts of saints who, thankfully were not killed for that purpose, are worshipped en masse by the believers and are not a personal fetish. Some of those saints must have had more hearts, fingers and toes than any human body can accommodate judging by their distribution around the world.

The advent of the dreadful HIV/AIDS epidemic

finally brought some of the traditional healers and the western medical practitioners together for the common good. Joint seminars were held so that each could appraise the others capability, so that the traditional healers could tell when to send patients for western medical treatment or HIV clinics and when the traditionalists could cope best with certain symptoms. It's a start. But the Swaziland I knew of laid back friendly people who loved to dance and sing was already vanishing under a yoke of sickness, oppression, and maladministration.

Opening Pandora's Box

The Paramount Chief

So, as the country celebrates its half century of independence, what has been the fate of Swaziland under the rule of King Mswati 111 the last absolute ruler in sub Saharan Africa? To know what has changed, you need to know what was there before. All the Swazis around me seemed somewhat reluctant to discuss the royal family or the secretive political shenanigans happening up north, which might indeed have proved dangerous. Possibly they were also in the dark and with no other means of finding anything out, I had spent six happy years in my own little rural backwater of the kingdom in some ignorance, experiencing a different culture, enjoying new friendships and the burgeoning relationship with Robin. Now it was time for a reality check so let's start with a little history.

When King Sobhuza died in 1982, he had been the world's longest reigning monarch with 62 years or 83 if you count his minority. His father Ngwane V had died in 1899 at the age of only 24 while dancing with his soldiers at the Incwala ceremony it's said, when Sobhuza, his chosen successor, was only a few months old. So his grandmother Labotsibeni acted as the Ndlovakati, (Queen Regent) during his long minority at a time when 63% of the country was in the hands of foreigners, mainly Europeans and Boers, for mineral exploitation or farming. To some extent, this might be due to that common clash of understanding between the Africans' use of, or more precisely, the usufruct of the nation's land and the concessionaires' concept of outright ownership in perpetuity, but mainly it was downright exploitation, especially after gold was discovered near Barberton in the northwest region in the 1870s. The whole country experienced unruly mayhem between the Boer and British concessionaires. The Swazis, meanwhile, were confined to native reserves.

A wise and powerful woman Labotsibeni dominated Swazi politics until Sobhuza's coming of age. She set about grooming the young Sobhuza to deal with these foreign powers by creating a school for him in the royal village, importing teachers to educate him in the ways of the foreign occupiers and sending him to Lovedale College in the Cape. Here he made contact with fellow black students who were to become the leaders of the ANC and black African states. She tried to redress the land question by finding the means to buy back some of the foreign owned settlements. This she did by creating the Lifa fund and getting all Swazi households to contribute which, in the conditions prevailing at that time, meant cattle, the local Swazi currency. Her preparations for him to assume the mantle of power were long and thorough and the problems he inherited for the survival of Swaziland as an independent entity proved formidable during the early part of his reign.

However, the uncertain future of Swaziland during that time in the early 20th century, coupled with little interference from colonial officials based in Pretoria who had presupposed the High Commission Territories (Botswana, Lesotho and Swaziland) would eventually be incorporated into South Africa, (a plan later shelved when the Nationalists developed their policy of apartheid) gave Sobhuza as Paramount Chief of the Swazis, a powerful incentive and opportunity to develop a strong sense of national identity. He attempted to keep traditional Swazi society, under the leadership of the Dlamini clan, functioning as a working whole in the face of western consumerism, economic development, urbanization and missionary education. Unlike other emerging African states, he had no need to concentrate on moulding different tribes into a national whole within the borders outside forces had imposed because the Swazis were one whole united tribe already. Since the early 19th century, when his ancestors had moved inland from present Mozambique, they had conquered or incorporated the tribes and clans they found there and established a more or less united country under the leadership of the Dlamini aristocracy. So instead, Sobhuza concentrated on cultural nationalism and set about trying to preserve the status quo of the aristocracy and commoners and the acceptance of certain rules, by strengthening those myths and traditional practices that had fallen and creating new ones.

In the 1930s, he was alarmed by the influence the missionaries were having on the young which, he felt, was denigrating Swazi culture and weakening his control and that of the royal house over Swazi youth. The traditions of rank and status were also being weakened by outside demands for Swazi labour, especially in the mines and on white farms and by Christian concepts of equality. To build support for the monarchy and "pride of race", he set about strengthening the almost moribund regimental age system (ibutho). These militarized age grades had previously been used for warfare, cattle raiding and agricultural labour and they recognised the authority of the King above all else. Although the first two aims were no more, Sobhuza still included traditional military training, tribute labour for the King and Chiefs, Swazi Law and Custom, attendance at ceremonial occasions and the strict rules which applied to the various age groups including when they had the right to marry and the rules of lobola and kuhlawula (which is a fine of five cows if you impregnate an unmarried woman). Needless to say, this last has fallen by the wayside long since. How it came to be part of Swazi Law and Custom in the first place is puzzling since the king doesn't marry his chosen bride until she is pregnant. Sobhuza encouraged sibhaka dancing, originally an energetic war dance, a bit like the Maori Haka with drums. Competitions of these dances have grown in popularity, second only to football. He elaborated the First Fruits festivities (common to many of the African Nguni tribes at harvest time as a thanksgiving to the ancestors for the well being of the tribe and a good harvest) into the unique Swaziland Incwala Ceremony that legitimises the role of the king and still takes place yearly to this day. When there is no King, as in the case of his minority, there is no incwala. To counter the influence of mission education he established national schools where these rules of the age regiments were taught. His most important achievement though, in 1957, was to have the Chiefs of the various regions, over 300 of them, put under his authority and not as paid agents of the colonial government in the usual manner of indirect rule. The Chieftain territories were then amalgamated into bigger regions of 55 areas called Tinkhundla. All ethnic Swazis are subject to their district Chiefs and must pay him tribute, feudal fashion, usually by free labour in return for the right to cultivate some land.

Any birth, marriage or death certificate, any legal document, driver's license, business contract, ID or bank loan must specify who their Chief is. Since the vast majority of the Swazi population are subsistence farmers and the right to farm Swazi Nation Land is granted only by the Chiefs, (a position usually inherited but approved by the King), this gave Sobhuza power and leverage over almost all his subjects. In fact, this development of Swazi culture subsequently proved a very potent political weapon.

So, while Paramount Chief until his coronation as King in 1968, he was left in overall charge of native matters under (unwritten) Swazi Law and Custom while other matters pertaining to the settlers or international policy for instance, were dealt with by the Legislative Assembly or the colonial government. The heads of the Police, the courts and education, to name but three, were expatriates in the employ of the British Government. Until independence, one could say, Swazis and Settlers led almost parallel lives. This racial discrimination included separation of facilities like schools and hospital wards or Swazis not being allowed in clubs and hotels where alcohol was served. On one occasion in 1959, when Sobhuza, was invited to the Shiselweni agricultural show, the committee had to entertain him in the local law court because he was not allowed in the hotel. It was not until 1961 that a law was passed outlawing all this discrimination.

After the end of WWII when Britain was left battered, impoverished and hungry, thoughts turned to using the colonies to reduce the vast debt of the war and the expense of their administration by developing them economically. Due to the dollar war debt, it made more economic sense to trade in sterling areas, ie. the empire, and to try to produce some food and income for the Mother Country. Agricultural development seemed the natural choice but was of little interest to the business sector with its uncertainties, slow, long term development and modest, if any, profit margins. The disastrous Ghanaian groundnut scheme immediately springs to mind. Swaziland however, proved more successful in that regard. With British government backing by means of long term loans, the Colonial (later Commonwealth) Development Corporation stepped in. In 1948, they bought 76,000 acres of mountainous freehold land in the northwest region and established forestry plantations, the caveat being that the ground should be unsuitable for growing maize. Another two plantations followed, together with a pulp mill. Company villages were also built with housing for staff, schools, medical and sporting facilities, roads and offices, utilities and communication. At Usutu, a workforce of 1,000 would involve supporting 10,000 of the population in one way or another.

Since capital was now available, further large scale developments like the all important sugar industry, citrus fruits, mining, canning, cotton and rice came into being together with their infrastructure.

Any further expansion would involve the use of Swazi Nation Land and that was under the jurisdiction of the Chiefs and ultimately the King. It also provided a vehicle for investment and land acquisition for the Swazi monarchy. Granting leases of such land for industrial expansion meant evicting people from the land they had farmed successfully for decades. Although he was regarded as Father of the Nation, Sobhuza had no hesitation in taking over land he wanted which is what happened to 200 homesteads involving 5,000 people round the Simunya area, for example, to expand the valuable sugar industry. They were not rehoused nor did they get compensation and mainly ended up having to work on the sugar plantations as poorly paid itinerant labourers, but it provide Sobhuza with an investment opportunity to get involved in large scale, profitable enterprises and acquire lucrative shares in return. He had established Tibiyo Taka Ngwane, the Swazi National Development Fund, in order, he said, to buy out foreign interests in essential businesses like sugar and forestry. Although every Swazi male contributed a cow and was therefore nominally a shareholder, it was administered by the royal family "in trust for the nation" and was not subject to any scrutiny. It now also holds shares of 20 – 40% (often more) of any industrial development or business. Population displacement has continued to date and privately owned land bought back was mostly not passed to the chiefs for the benefit of the population but has enabled those in the royal house and a small elite to accumulate land and vast wealth.

The Absolute Ruler

During the early 60s various political parties within Swaziland were jostling for power and demanding independence and economic reform. In 1963 there was a strike at the Havelock Asbestos Mine of Swazi trade unionists flexing their political muscles and spreading unrest to other parts. This was put down by the colonial government in a fairly peaceful manner by some 300 soldiers of the Ist Battalion Gordon Highlanders brought in from Kenya. Apart from the striking miners, they were, in fact, quite popular with the general Swazi public since they, like the Swazis, wore skirts, (kilts) played the bagpipes and danced the Highland Fling. They also built roads, bridges, left behind a field hospital and a very useful blood bank. However, the main problem with the opposition to the hardline traditionalists was, and is, their fragmentation. Proposals for a sort of race federation were put forward within Swaziland, supported by Sobhuza and given propaganda and financial help by South Africa. This would leave the settlers with their way of voting and the traditional Tinkhundla system for the Swazi. This system started at the grass roots level for some of the posts with 4 men nominated by the district residents, approved by the chiefs and the winner decided by the counting of heads as voters passed through one of the four gates where each candidate stood. As my students

189

remarked, you thereby make one friend and three enemies and need to take care who you antagonize. It was not until the 1990s that voter registration and secret ballots were introduced. The leaders of both the Legislative and the Tinkundla system were, of course, reluctant to let go any of their power. Here I find the Swazi position a little confusing since they would have far outnumbered the rest of the population anyway with a democratic one man, one vote and Sobhuza was to have been left with a veto, control of the mining and property revenue and the right to appoint the chief justice. Nevertheless, at that point, he seemed to prefer half a loaf of absolute control over his own people, leaving the small minority of settlers their privileged positions rather than give up any of his regal power. However, the colonial powers argued against the status quo. A two way federation would leave out a growing section of educated, detribalized, urban, politicized Swazis and mixed race people. It would also strengthen apartheid South Africa's philosophy of separate development, whereas the British, with an eye on the goodwill of the other African newly independent colonial territories, no doubt, were anxious to show that multicultural government was a workable model. In preparation, they had already passed anti discrimination legislation in 1961. So, at independence in 1968, when Sobhuza was

190

acknowledged as King, the colonial powers left Swaziland with a system neither side wanted; a Westminster type government consisting of a constitutional monarchy, power resting in the parliament elected by the people, the freedom for political parties and trade unions to exist, freedom of speech and assembly and an independent judiciary. They had used the same model with the other two protectorates of Botswana and Lesotho. Sobhuza reluctantly formed his own political party and swept to power winning every seat. It was after the subsequent Swazi election in 1973 when the opposition gained 20% of votes and 3 seats in parliament that Sobhuza got alarmed. An opposition could question policies, bring up the land ownership problem and challenge his leadership powers, so he declared a state of emergency, repealed the constitution, dissolved parliament, banned political parties, barred trade unions and assumed all powers of government. His appointees were essentially aristocratic, with a council of elders and (at that time) an advisory council called the liqoqo while the King was head over all. Although he kept an outward semblance of government with Parliament consisting of a House of Assembly and the Senate, there were to be no political parties and in essence all members had to be approved or appointed by the King and elections were competitions for patronage, not policies. He justified his actions by declaring,

"Alien political practices are incompatible with the Swazi way of life."

The state of emergency has never been repealed.

As Paramount Chief, before Independence, Sobhuza had aimed at ruling the majority ethnic Swazi population according to traditional Swazi Law and custom for the last half century, leaving its traditionalism largely intact and even strengthened. It has been suggested that the decision was strongly encouraged and even helped by the SA Nationalist Government who were alarmed by the newly independent, democratic, leftward leaning African states around them and found it easier to deal with and influence a single, conservative despotic ruler and his cabal than an entire population with their own views of how the country should be run.

Although by the time of independence, thanks in large part to the late Labotsibeni and help from the British government, the amount of foreign owned land in Swaziland had decreased from 63% to 34%, Sobhuza inherited a country that was still little more than half the size of that of his grandfather. More ethnic Swazis lived outside the "agreed" borders of almost a century ago than inside. It had always been his ambition to recover that territory (irrespective of whether their populations wished to become part of a feudal kingdom and lose their right to South African citizenship), with numerous unsuccessful petitions to the British government. It subsequently proved to be his achilles heel in his dealings with South Africa. With the advent of the Nationalist Government in South Africa, the spread of the apartheid bantustan policy and the protests of the protectorates, to put it simply, incorporation into South Africa was no longer appropriate and the independence of the BLS states was inevitable.

Sobhuza, even as king, lived an ascetic, simple lifestyle largely declining Western consumerism, unlike his successor, and was a man of the people. According to those who met him on social occasions, he was greeted with a bow from both his Swazi and his foreign guests. Once when the directors of the Swaziland Development and Savings Bank, consisting mainly of Swazis and a couple of expatriates, wanted to make him a present of a grandfather clock, he met them personally, barefooted, wearing only a traditional sarong and the royal head feathers and had them wandering from room to room trying out various positions for the clock until he was satisfied where he wanted it placed. Some people remembered that when invited to an official dinner, he would sit and eat and chat with the rest of the company. There were other times when Swazi situations called for full traditional formality. Brig. John Gray, employed to organise Swaziland's first regular army, Umbutfo Swaziland Defence Force (USDF) in "Climbing the Army Ladder" writes of his astonishment, when summoned to the palace, on seeing the Prime Minister, Major General Maphevu Dlamini, approaching the King on hands and knees. Crawling to the king like this is something that happens a great deal more often these days.

But Sobhuza could be both flexible and accessible. His many wives, believed to total about 70, lived in (mainly) traditional Swazi houses in the royal village and wore the traditional clothes of married Swazi women of black leather pleated skirts, beehive hairstyles and a cloth across one shoulder. They kept a low profile and tended not to leave the royal village, but if they needed to, Sobhuza would transport his huge family by buses, not a fleet of BMWs and private jets like the present King. Nor did they indulge in high fashion and go on frequent extravagant shopping trips to Vegas or Paris etc., which might be slightly more acceptable if the majority of his successor Mswati's 111 subjects were not living on less than two dollars a day and more than 65% dependent on food aid from the rest of the world just to stay alive. But nevertheless, Sobhuza's idealization of Swazi cultural activities, the rejection of anything deemed un-Swazi, amounted to a manipulation of the culture for political gain since the arbiter of what was Swazi, rested with him and his circle. He could make it mean anything he wanted. All offers by UN agencies to help Swaziland regularize and write down what constituted Swazi Laws and Customs were met with refusals. There was also, of course, a big difference in the effect of this on the country when Sobhuza was Paramount Chief dealing separately with Swazi laws for Swazi people and after independence when dual laws and a multiethnic, multicultural population together were involved in the process of government

We come back once more to the matter of Tibyo Taka Ngwane. At independence in 1968, the country the colonials left behind was prosperous, peaceful and pretty stable. All the assets and rents, including mineral rights that had previously accrued to the colonial government should have been passed over to the Treasury but at Sobhuza's insistence, they were handed over to Tibiyo, the fund he had set up for "the benefit of the nation." Tibiyo, not the government, receives the royalties from mining, sugar, land development and the shares it owns in almost every enterprise, anything from 20-40% or even more. It is totally secretive, above the law, not subject to any scrutiny, doesn't pay taxes and for "Wealth of the Nation" read slush fund for the royal family. Not even the IMF could get it to open its

195

books. But one Minister took them on.

In 1979, to everyone's surprise, Sobhuza, perhaps realizing the need for change, appointed Prince Mabandla as his Prime Minister. He was a plant manager with no political experience but with a reputation as a good administrator and a man of integrity. He put this to use almost immediately by appointing a commission of enquiry into allegations of corruption and bribery. This not only alarmed Sobhuza's most powerful circle when some of its more prominent members came under scrutiny, particularly Mfanasibili, but when Mabandla also wanted to open the finances of Tibiyo for inspection thereby clashing with its director, Sishayi Nxumalo, the second most powerful man in the kingdom, the King realized his PM would have to be reigned in. Since he was very popular with the Swazi public and could hardly be dismissed for being honest and conscientious, Sobhuza appointed two powerful hardline traditionalist Ministers to create a balance. The biggest clash though happened when Mabandla was not in support of acquiring the KaNgwane bantustan land that the South Africans were offering.

As a way of getting rid of its black African majority and trying to make South Africa a white man's country, it gave the forced homelands it had created their "independence" which the rest of the world refused to recognize. Swaziland was different since it was already a recognized kingdom, so to enlarge it by adding 900,000 of the Republic's unwanted ethnic Swazis, might have a certain legitimacy. Mabandla didn't think gaining another third of land and an outlet to the sea, but more than doubling Swaziland's population was such a hot idea. It would look as though Swaziland had sold out, rejected the ideals of the liberation struggle (although Sobhuza had been one of the founder members of the ANC), and become an accomplice of the South African government and its policies. Its standing in the international community, including the OAU, would suffer and a huge influx of population who did not necessarily share Swaziland's conservative traditional beliefs or restrictions on land ownership, were politically more sophisticated and a large percentage of whom were displaced and unemployed, might destabilize the country. In any case, some of the land on offer was not contiguous with the Swazi border. It was separated by a swathe of white owned farmland some twenty miles wide, which was not part of the arrangement. The secret deal remained unratified but Sobhuza took steps to control his PM and parliament. In 1982 he upgraded the informal advisory role of the liqoqo to the Supreme Council of State with virtually unlimited powers "to overrule any law or decision not in the national interest." Members were to be appointed by the king or Queen Mother, in this case Dzeliwe, whom he had just appointed as Regent. Swazi kings do not appoint their successor but the Queen Regent is a different matter. As part of the unwritten constitution, the Queen or Queen Regent is the other half of Swaziland's dual monarchy, the she elephant to the king's lion, the keeper of the royal regalia and rain making power. She is in charge with the help of advisors until a crown prince comes of age at twenty one and ascends the throne when his own mother takes over the role. With the land situation still unresolved, Sobhuza died in August 1982 and vicious internecine fighting immediately broke out in the royal household. The King had always been the indisputable voice of authority, successfully keeping the country and the royal house stable while walking a tightrope between the traditionalists and the modernizers within his house, not to mention negotiating with the powerful RSA, but as soon as he was gone, stability went with him.

The Teenage King

The main concern of the Liqoqo was to get rid of Mabandla as soon as possible but he was a hard man to shift despite (alleged) assassination attempts and the use of witchcraft. The Queen Regent, Dzeliwe supported him and refused to sign his dismissal notice. Like herself, he had been put in place by the late king himself and to go against his wishes almost amounted to treason in her eyes. The response by the Liqoqo was to steal the Queen's regalia of office, her proof of power and get rid of them both, which they did. They made the pro South African Prince Bhekimpi Prime Minister, named the 14 year old Prince Makosetive (later Mswati 111) as Sobhuza's successor and declared his mother Mtombi as the Queen Regent, although her son had neither gained his majority nor his throne by this time. Neither did Mtombi have the status usually required of a mother of a future King if the US Ambassador, Earl Irvine's, allegation (exposed by Wikileaks) of her position as maid to one of Sobhuza's wives and a posthumous marriage to Sobhuza' corpse are to be believed. Unrest broke out in the country, the University students came out on strike and PUDEMO, and various other movements for democracy held protest rallies. In response Bhekimpi closed the university, ordered draconian public order measures and issued a statement telling the protesters they should "Accept

199

with gratitude the direction the elders have mapped out for the country" and arrested those who didn't.

In 1984 he signed another secret treaty for the acquisition of the Kgwane land that South Africa offered. That was the carrot. The whip was Swaziland agreeing to purge their territory of anti apartheid "aliens" and ANC activists who had taken refuge in the kingdom and which the army, police and SA forces duly carried out with killings, kidnappings, car bombs and much brutality particularly around the Manzini region and the border with Mozambique, causing the ANC to relocate further north in Zambia. They were actions which were likely to have lasting consequences when the ANC finally formed the government of South Africa. Meanwhile, the rumours flying around Nhlangano at that time of bodies driven across the border at night could have been only too true. Once the Republic had achieved their real aim and also signed the non aggression Nkomati Accord with Mozambique, whereby they also expelled the ANC in return for South Africa not arming the MNR, (also subsequently ignored) the promise of land was dropped but the damage to Swaziland's reputation had already been done.

But the internal quarreling and maneuvering got worse over the next few years with palace uprisings and imprisonments condemning one faction then another. The only way to resolve this, according to the palace powers, seemed to be to have a King in charge, bring the prince home from his school in the UK and bring his coronation forward by three years. So, Makhosetive suddenly found himself, at the age of eighteen, the world's youngest monarch, brought to the throne as Mswati 111 with unseemly haste by political intrigue for the sake of stability within the royal house. Fifteen of the group who had overthrown Dzeliwe were charged with treason and given long prison sentences which were commuted some months later (except for Mfanasibili, the chief instigator). The liqoqo was subsequently dissolved and the hope was that the country could return to the peaceful, prosperous state in which Sobhuza had left it. A vain hope as it turned out.

Catapulting an untried teenager into the role of absolute monarch, notwithstanding the help and advice from those around him, was like putting a child into a toy shop of his own and telling him he could help himself to anything and everything, which Mswati promptly did and has never stopped. By the time of his 50th birthday in 2018, he had accumulated 13 palaces, more than 50 top of the range cars, one a Maybach for half a million, two aeroplanes, a dining and lounge set of gold, a suit studied with diamonds, a wristwatch worth one and a half million dollars and enough wealth to put him in

201

the top ten of the world's richest kings.

To make allowances, Mswati 111 had none of the advantages of his father for preparing him for his role. A successor to the kingship from among his many wives is not decided while the king is alive and could be one of a number of siblings, though the stipulation that he should be the only son of his mother does narrow it down. Sobhuza had had long years of preparation for the role dominated by the charismatic Nodlovokasi Labotsibeni who struggled hard for the welfare of her people and taught Sobhuza to do the same. Mswati on the other hand, at fourteen years of age was plucked from comparative obscurity by the decision of the liqoqo, who thought he would be easy to manipulate, and then sent out of the way abroad to an English public school for the next few years. Whatever he might have learnt there, it was not how to be the responsible leader of the Swazi nation or a man of the people. Then, instead of giving him a further three years to mature into the position till his coming of age at 21 as Swazi law and custom dictated, this 18 year old was catapulted into the kingship with an elaborate coronation and handed two official wives for good measure.

One of his first acts, typical of a teenager, was to invite his friends from school in England and show off his new found status, his kingdom and his wives. Not bad, he (and they) must have thought, for a chap they just called Mac at school. As amply demonstrated by his 50/50 party, this habit of showing off didn't unfortunately wane with maturity. Not only does the king control over 60% of the land as Swazi Nation Land but through Tibiyo he owns a percentage of all the minerals, real estate, breweries, insurance, media and mobile phones, the sugar industry and agricultural products. It amounts to many million dollars on top of the very substantial income which he and his family are granted by Parliament. This, added to the very considerable amount his father left, are what put him in the top ten of the world's richest rulers. But, never raised with any expectations and owing his position to others in the royal family meant, to begin with, having to stay on good terms with them and a first class recipe for nepotism and corruption. The need to rely on a royal clique may have made his position a little precarious, if not dangerous, which might explain his strong belief in witchcraft for protection and some of the royal practices he revived like the royal taster to see he doesn't get poisoned or the collector of royal hair, toe and finger nails etc so they cannot be used in witchcraft against him. I'm told the chair the King has sat on during official country engagements in Swaziland has to be destroyed, presumably so that no one else can claim that privilege. One would have thought it made more sense to have his own exclusive chair taken around, one of his gold ones, perhaps? It might also go some way to explaining why His Majesty decided he must have a second, more luxurious plane for his frequent foreign travelling to include not only a state room but his own personal toilet. In spite of officially being Christian and professing to get messages directly from God, there is great reliance on muti and sangomas against danger in the royal household and a powerful sangoma from Mozambique in residence. Any slight tummy upset or being unwell is immediately put down to poisoning and accusations of witchcraft. One of his wives had to make a hasty exit to the UK for three months till the accusations of having poisoned him died down. Shaking hands is forbidden, widows are not allowed in his presence and he must sit elevated above his subjects while they crawl to him on hands and knees. On one occasion when delegates wanted to meet with a reluctant king, they had to sit on the floor, as usual, while he occupied the chair. Then the underfloor heating was turned on high but, despite cooking, no one dared to protest or get up and leave. That taught them a lesson; think twice before you bother the boss with your problems. Praise singers accompany him everywhere as does a huge entourage on his frequent trips abroad.

At a recent 2017 Indo – African Trade Mission in

Delhi, whereas the other 50 or so African nations invited turned up with just their foreign or trade ministers and some with their heads of state, Mswati was said to have turned up with several wives, 30 of his family and more than 100 servants and officials in tow. 200 rooms in the most expensive five star hotel in Delhi were engaged, each room costing more per night than the average Swazi earns in a year. When the Indian papers reported this pomp and extravagance at their taxpayers' expense, the response of the local Swazi press, which is owned by the king, was an angry " lies, all lies." In 2011 on the occasion of Prince William's wedding to Kate Middleton, when the Swazi government didn't have enough money in the treasury to pay the public sector wage bill, the King, nevertheless, took a party of 50 to London at vast expense, staying at one of the most expensive hotels for a week. Any journalist who is critical of the King is likely to join those already imprisoned without trial. Nor is this kind of jamboree an isolated event. The King rarely misses an opportunity to show off his personal wealth or his imagined importance, taking part, entourage in tow, in any commemorations, celebrations, commonwealth or international meetings in various parts of the world, speaking at the UN and being photographed with world leaders of which he counts himself as one.

If he thinks this kind of behaviour is admired or envied by the rest of the world he is sadly mistaken but that is not the point. It reinforces the image he wants to create among his own people as an important, powerful man and Swaziland, which he embodies, as a world player. Since, with draconian censorship, they are never allowed to see or hear anything to the contrary that is, one presumes, what they come to believe. He also alleges since God has spoken to him and directed his decisions for the nation on several occasions, they must be the right ones.

Unfortunately, despite the reinforcing rituals of the Incwala ceremony and the Reed festival, economic reality is fast putting paid to the myth of the all powerful, important King. Following the economic surpluses of the 1970s and 80s, the 1990s on saw Swaziland's economic growth lagging behind its other African neighbours and the surplus fast disappearing. One reason was and is the overblown size of government employees, (40% of the workforce) and massive corruption running at twice the social services budget which loses the treasury an estimated 960 million rand a year. In 2016 International auditors Kobla Quashie Consultants reported $360 million missing from government funds possibly due, they said, to maladministration, corruption or even embezzlement.

During the apartheid years, the RSA suppressed the development of local industries in the BLS states (Botswana, Lesotho and Swaziland) like TV assembly, fertiliser production, hessian bags etc., trying to force them to recognise the bantustans. They relocated many businesses there and gave them massive subsidies which undercut what the BLS states were able to charge for their goods and services (like Nhlangano's shirt factory) and so drove them out of business. After Nelson Mandela's release, economic sanctions against SA were dropped, gambling was no longer banned and the immorality act repealed, all of which had given Swaziland an economic advantage. Then, apart from the overblown and inefficient government sector already mentioned, whose wage bill takes up almost 55% of public spending and the obscene extravagance of the royal household, there was also the spectre of HIV/AIDS.

It first appeared in Swaziland in the late 80s and given the sexual practices of Swazi men, subordinate position of women, high prevalence of rape and the banning of birth control clinics, it spread uncontrolled like wildfire leaving Swaziland with the highest per capita toll in Africa, if not the world, at over 33%. With the co-infection of TB, according to the UN figures the life expectancy halved from 61 in 2000 to 32 years in 2009. The highest increase of the disease was among girls in the 15–19 age group, no doubt exacerbated by the rumours that sex with a virgin will cure AIDS. The death toll of parents has left a legacy of 230,000 orphaned and vulnerable children, almost a quarter of the total population which the state, with help from outside agencies, is supposed to take care of, but too often falls short driving many into prostitution or people trafficking gangs. Although Swaziland, as usual, signed all the UN acts against trafficking in people in 2009, according to a survey by the US Department of State, "The (Swazi) government did not convict anyone on trafficking charges for the sixth consecutive year." In fact, some of the sex workers brave enough to speak out, claim the police themselves are among the offenders. As for implementing the UN act against forced labour, in 2017, the Ministry of Education postponed the opening of all schools, including primary, so the children could finish weeding the fields of the King, his wives and the chiefs!

Only 22% of Swazi children grow up in a 2 parent family and 50% of the population is under 18. A huge proportion of households are child led and with women over 60 only 5% of the population, grannies, the traditional child carers, are in short supply and struggling to cope with the huge numbers left in their care with no household wage earners.

Despite all that, there was still a reluctance to talk

openly about sexual issues. A sizable proportion of parents still object to the subject being brought into the school curriculum arguing that only total abstinence would solve the problem of AIDS. In an atmosphere of fear and denial all sorts of rumours as to the cause were given an airing: it was spread by monkeys, by condoms, infected oranges, even bizarrely, by hair curlers! Needless to say, many alleged it was due to witchcraft, but 1/3 still thought that traditional healers could cure it. The low status of women meant husbands or sexual partners had control and often refused any kinds of precaution. A sizable proportion of men married under monogamous Common Law also still had a number of extramarital partners and brought AIDS back home. Life expectancy dropped to 48.

The economic toll on the country of the epidemic has also contributed to its decline. Qualified and experienced civil servants, trained teachers and scientists, nurses and even doctors are dying. Sometimes up to half the workforce is lost and with it efficiency and expertise, not to mention the financial losses due to sickness, expensive traditional Swazi funerals and the retraining of new manpower. As the director of the UN Development Programme said in 2009,

"The longer term existence of Swaziland as a country will be seriously threatened."

The king took some time coming to terms with the problem. Now, more than a quarter of a century after its arrival, he pledges that he will personally stamp out HIV/AIDS by 2022, the date by which he has promised to turn Swaziland into a first world nation! This was received with wild cheering in Parliament and disbelief elsewhere. Neither did he venture to say how he would achieve it. He had previously proposed other ways of tackling the epidemic. In 2000, to everyone's horror, he suggested victims should be sterilized and branded. In 2001 he went down the traditional route by reviving umcwasho, a decree whereby young girls under 18 should abstain from sex for five years announcing the fact that they are virgins and out of bounds by wearing a colourful woolen halter-like neck band (umcwasho). They were also forbidden to shake hands with men or to wear trousers. Many thought it was a joke. When the king attended a degree ceremony at the university, not a single umcwasho was to be seen. Draw your own conclusion. Annoyed, he instituted a fine of R150 or one cow payable for breaching the law and sent soldiers into schools to winkle out transgressors. This so called solution, of course, reinforces the control over young Swazi women and puts the responsibility for controlling AIDS on their shoulders. Not that they have much say in it. They have no voice. Sexual abuse and incest are all too common and go mostly unreported. Wife beating is not an offense and marital rape is not even recognised. The men, meanwhile, added to the takings of prostitutes and brought even more AIDS back to their families. Back street abortions were on the rise and so was rape, since virginity had been so clearly signposted for the men who believed sex with a virgin would cure them. The king almost immediately broke his own rule by taking a 17 year old as his next wife and fined himself a cow. His next idea was to pay the girls not to have sex but that was doomed to failure. Efforts among men to encourage circumcision which some thought would reduce the incidence of AIDS had a very limited take up as did the use of condoms. Not only were there conflicting reports for and against circumcision but rumours spread that the foreskins would be used as muti in witchcraft to make them sterile.

However, the incidence of HIV/AIDS, with the joint efforts of NGOs, churches, UN agencies and the government, has shown a decline with the use of antiretroviral drugs, the lowering of mother to baby infection, testing now available in every health clinic and sex education and publicity given priority. The major sticking points though are still the subordinate role of women who are not in charge of their own decision making, older men passing the infection to young girls and the stigma attached to HIV/AIDS.

Forced under aged marriages, with some girls as young as 13, allowed by Swazi Law and Custom also play their part.

 Poverty too makes the fight back harder especially when the government runs out of funds to pay suppliers of the necessary drugs and run the clinics. Also, on top of a series of poor annual rainfalls, reduced harvests and 40,000 cattle that families relied on dying, people were less able to feed themselves on land that is overcrowded, overgrazed and often without adult workers available. Since they have no title to the land and the government has refused help to establish drip feed or any other kind of irrigation systems, the King declaring that "God will provide the irrigation", they have to rely solely on rainfall, which failed them during the El Nino weather cycle. Meanwhile, the irrigation systems for the sugar and other industries which provide Tybio with large profits, are given priority. That leaves 65% of the population depending on food aid from international donors.

When Japan donated 12,000 tonnes of Maize to feed those in need, Parliament sold it off for $3m and put the money in a special bank account, an act that was not made public. Nor was that the only occasion according to a ministerial whistle-blower. Later justification for this action by the Minister responsible was that people must learn to be self

212

reliant and not depend on handouts! Meanwhile, more handouts, i.e. international food donations, were left to rot in the warehouses at Matsapha because the government couldn't organise their distribution, either because there were no lorries available or it couldn't find the money for petrol! Since the government has so little regard for the welfare of its own people, it would seem sensible for the Aid agencies to have some of their own trusted personnel in place to collect and distribute the consignments of food as they arrive and get them to the right people. Unfortunately the "right" people are often the Chiefs of the area, some of whom use the distribution of food aid as yet another means of reinforcing their power base. I'm often asked why the Swazis don't simply rebel, but since 70% of the population are rural workers dependent on the Chiefs, the eyes and ears of the King, for the allocation of land to cultivate which forms their sole means to earn a living, they have to support the status quo. Swazis are good workers of the land. If you gave them title they would be able to get bank loans to develop their land and help in times of drought, but leave them at the mercy of uncertain rainfall and there isn't much they can do about it. Create more co-operatives for the joint use of agricultural machinery and actually keep it in working order and they could produce a great deal more than digging the land with a hoe.

Undaunted, the King was agitating for his parliament to authorize the purchase of a private jet for the royal journeys at a cost of $11million. Even the rubber stamp parliament objected to this use of public funds when they couldn't even pay the public sector wages and refused.

At one point, South Africa was approached for a rescue loan for the treasury shortfall but since it came with democratic reforms attached, the King turned it down. But in 2012, the jet appeared anyway after a further luxurious interior outfitting bringing the cost to US$18 million; a birthday present, the king said, from a mysterious benefactor he refused to name. When it was impounded in Canada for unpaid bills for the upgrade, the 'birthday present' was revealed as something else entirely. The international community, but not the Swazis, were treated to an unsavoury saga of friendships turning sour and the murky world of Swazi business deals. We have come a long way since the days 100 years ago when presents of crates of gin and some greyhounds earned you concession rights from the King. Nowadays, it is more in the form of a jet aeroplane and 40% shares in the enterprise as happened with 'benefactor' Shah's company, Sagaocor. After the King refused to honour the repayment of loans of several millions to SG Air, also owned by Shah, for the modifications of the plane, the cost of an upgrade to a better hire plane in the interim because the one offered only had one toilet, plus the return of an advance of $10 million to the King against future profits of Shah's iron ore company Sagaocor when the company ran into difficulties, relations with his 'birthday' friend turned very sour. The result was predictable. The King forced the company to close without compensation, putting 700 people out of work, while Shah took to the courts and got P.Id and vilified in the Swazi press for his pains. The message this gives to any potential international investors seems entirely to have passed Mswati by. Reputable investment firms need the certainty of legally binding contracts, not royal whims.

The Swazi government tried to persuade the Canadian court that Mswati had diplomatic immunity, but that didn't wash because the plane was registered to the King's private company. So the Swazi government had to pay $3.5 million surety and in 2016, the King promptly demanded a bigger and more luxurious A340 Airbus seating 300 and costing $30 million. Parliament, having declared a state of emergency in 2015 and begging the world for food aid for its starving population, had the temerity to turn down the request, protesting that in the present financial crises it didn't have the means for yet another royal plane. What was the need for a royal plane with room for 300 anyway? The king retaliated by refusing to sign the budget or any other act into law, forcing the country to a stand still until they did a U turn and granted a downpayment to the Taiwanese firm selling it. Why one of the world's richest men does not pay for these indulgences himself instead of the taxpayer and laying himself open to vilification is hard to understand. It would scarcely make a dent in the billions he has squirreled away in Saudi Arabian or other overseas banks.

So now we have progressed from the king's fleet of expensive cars including a Maybach for half a million, which, to stop the protests of the public, they are forbidden to photograph; thirteen palaces for his wives, a private jet, and an international airport he had built in the remote north east of the country at a cost of more than a billion dollars and named after himself and which needs 300,000 to 400,000 passengers p.a. to cover its running and construction costs. This is opposed to the 70,000 pa maximum who used to arrive at the original airport at Matsapha. Where the extra numbers needed to cover costs are coming from is far from clear. No preliminary needs analysis was done and there are plenty of more convenient airports available nearby at Maputo, Nelspruit, Durban and Jo'burg. No international airline was signed up to use the new airport and it seems that none will. Only Swaziland

Airlink, jointly owned by Swaziland and SAA, uses it to fly to Jo'burg with less than 150 passengers a day. The King himself doesn't use it, preferring to fly from the old airport at Matsapha which he turned over to the army. It is actually quicker now to travel to Jo'burg by car than make your way to remote KMA and fly.

However, this remote white elephant of an airport did come into its own in 2016 when the Big Game Parks of Swaziland sold 18 real elephants to various zoos in the US for $450,000; trucked them, under sedation, to a holding area for 26 hours and hurriedly flew them, still drugged and crated for a further 24 hours, the 9,000 miles to the US from King Mswati Airport in a 727 while legal proceedings by various animal charities to stop them were still under way. The number of elephants was revised from 18 down to 17 with no explanation. The reason given for the sale was the drought sweeping across southern Africa which caused the animals to degrade their habitat in search of food to the detriment of the rhino. The elephant population of 40, they said, was too great for the land in the modest wildlife parks available for them.

But since pre independence Swaziland had been denuded by farmers of any remaining wildlife of its own, due to the policy of culling to stop the spread of tick borne diseases to their domestic herds. All the

217

BGP variety of wild animals had been imported in the 1980s and 90s, mainly from South Africa to add another attraction to their tourist industry which thrived at that time. Swaziland then was seen as a haven of peace, good for holidays while there were ongoing sanctions against the Republic and civil unrest in Mozambique. However, BGP had previously sold 11 elephants to US zoos back in 2003 for hundreds of thousands of dollars before the present severe drought could be used as an excuse. Since the present herd is kept in elephant proof fenced areas separate from the rhino, might it not have been feasible to move or increase the fenced areas or even let them migrate to find their own food? After the first sale in 2003, it would perhaps have been sensible to work out how many these small parks can comfortably accommodate and to limit the elephant population by birth control without culling or condemning them to a life of captivity. Allowing the 19 imported into Swaziland originally in the 80s to increase to the present 40, not even counting those sold previously, smacks of commercialism. Threatening to kill the 18 elephants if they were not allowed to be exported to US zoos smacks of blackmail. In any case, I don't believe BGP would risk world wide condemnation by killing 18 healthy animals. Elephants live in family groups and to break them up for the sake of exhibiting them in zoos is cruel in the extreme. Acknowledging that fact, many world class zoos including London, Bristol and Longleat have given up keeping elephants in captivity as morally repugnant. Far from rescuing the elephants, BGP appears to be harming one species for the sake of another more lucrative, in this case, the rhino.

Swaziland shocked the world of conservation by proposing to sell off, to some Eastern nation (probably its friend and ally Taiwan which is not recognized by the UN and therefore not part of CITES) its stockpile of rhino horn, taken, they said, from illegal poachers and animals that had died, for some $9.9 million. But they also wanted to farm rhino horn, which demands higher prices than gold, pound for pound, by regularly darting the animals and cutting their horns. This would mean breaking the international CITES agreement on endangered species which has been in place since 1977, but which South Africa only signed in 2009. During those thirty years, rhino horn farming flourished internally in the Republic. John Hume, a Zimbabwean who moved to the Republic, farms the biggest herd of 1,600, which would make him one of the richest men in Southern Africa if the CITES ban was lifted, and he was also allowed to sell off his stockpile worldwide.

The Swazis said the money raised from their rhino

horns would be earmarked to pay for further conservation, but given the value of the trade, the level of government corruption and remembering the fate of some of the food aid intended for the starving population, I don't hold out much hope for that happening. To make sure his starving peasants didn't take it into their heads to poach anything to eat, the King armed and granted immunity from prosecution to BGP's Ted Reilly and his rangers if they shot dead anyone trying to do just that which, of course, they did on occasions even when the alleged poachers were unarmed. In Swaziland even the life of a warthog is obviously more valuable than the life of one of its citizens.

So what next on the King's agenda for this little, impoverished landlocked country? A deep sea port no less! They would dig a canal of 26 km from Mlawula in Swaziland to the Mozambique coast deep enough for the large ships Durban and Maputo were (allegedly) too shallow to handle. The new port would outshine them both. It was not a hoax, the Minister of Commerce, Trade and Industry Gideon Dlamini told reporters. There were one or two obstacles, of course but those could be overcome.

First, as critics have pointed out, the distance wasn't 26km but 70km. A slight miscalculation admitted the Minister. Then there was the question of passing through land that rises sharply and would need a series of locks, a major engineering task of horrendous expense."No problem, it will be dealt with." Land acquisition? Sweeping the peasants off their land was never a problem in Swaziland. It didn't belong to them anyway. Cutting through Mlawula Nature Reserve? A little more of a problem but the King would solve it. Of course he would.

Since Mozambique has been kept unaware of this project officially, wouldn't it be a good idea to ask them for permission to build an enormous shipping canal across their land to the sea?

"Ah well," said the Minister of Commerce, Gideon Dlamini, "You must understand that the project is in phases and the stage of engaging Mozambique is still in the pipeline".

And if they say "No" as they did to the Malawi/Zambezi port project for "putting popular politics before achievable, realistic goals," what then? Would the government use some of the billions earmarked for this project to reverse the cut in teachers and civil servants' salaries, the loss of pension rights, aid to the old, cuts in school equipment and food, the shortfall of drugs and medical supplies, get ambulances and tractors repaired and functioning, develop an adequate water supply, clean up the hospitals and feed the starving etc.,etc? Balanced against an Airbus 340, I have my doubts. Following an official visit of the King and

221

his entourage to Mozambique in 2016, nothing more has been heard to date of the deep canal scheme to the sea.

In spite of all this one feels many Swazis are still proud to have a monarch and the country people in particular adhere to the notion "the King was given by God", but the majority would like to demarcate the king's powers and make the monarchy more accountable. Building on the efforts of the indomitable Nlovakasi Labotsibeni, Sobhuza, although an authoritarian dictator, gave the Swazis back their dignity, their respect and together with major foreign investment, made visible improvements to their standard of living with schools, jobs, roads and medical facilities, so it probably didn't matter much to the rural majority if they had political voting rights or not when the country was so prosperous. On the whole, they were happy to leave the running of the country in the hands of the King.

That residue of respect has allowed the present King Mswati to get away with much that would have overthrown most leaders. Some people have tended to blame poor counseling by his advisors or members of Parliament rather than Mswati himself "the mouth that tells no lies" though even that belief is wearing thin. More and more are beginning to realise that he seems to regard his people as enemies to be coerced and restrained by ever more brutal methods while he goes on spending and spending. In 2008 he told his PM to crack down on terrorism. Human rights and social conditions declined and freedom of speech and assembly were restricted, but it is difficult to measure the strength of the opposition since any protest is brutally suppressed under the label of terrorism and many have fled across the border seeking sanctuary in South Africa, operating their opposition from outside the country and bringing the wheel full circle.

Musa Hlophe summed up the feelings of the young exiles when he said,

"We wanted a country where we were seen as proper citizens and not just lowly subjects".

Terrorism is anything the King regards as criticism. Apart from the more obvious opposition of the banned Trade Unions and PUDEMO, the movement for democracy, just the wearing of T shirts with anti establishment slogans is enough to get you beaten up or arrested. Even church meetings, funerals or educational workshops have been broken up by the military.

Swaziland has no external enemies, so it's hard to understand why the King would want to import millions of dollars worth of heavy military weaponry. The UK wondered the same thing in 2011 when it blocked the shipment of weapons to the kingdom amid concerns of their end use. Why would the government require armoured personnel carriers fitted with machine guns, 1,000 assault rifles of various sorts, military ambulances, ground to air missiles, helicopters, submachine guns and semi automatic pistols, water cannons and tear gas? A government spokesman pleaded cattle rustling problems on its Mozambique border. Given the absurdity of that explanation, it then got changed to needing them for its UN peacekeeping role when its turn came, which didn't prove an adequate explanation either. Despite the embargo, they managed to import the weaponry from elsewhere anyway and had no compunction about using it on their own citizens. Rubber bullets, water cannon and tear gas are used liberally to disperse any meetings of protest, so much so, they actually ran out of tear gas. In early 2016 when University students were protesting about delays in registration and payments of grants, police armoured vehicles were used to drive at speed among the students, running them down if they didn't scatter fast enough which left many injured and Ayanda Mkhabela paralysed and never able to walk again. By giving the army and the police immunity from prosecution, the King has unleashed a brutality that knows no bounds: torture and deaths in custody, long pretrial detentions, mob killings, beatings, killings to order, violence against women and children, people trafficking, kidnappings and total disregard for any law.

Just about every international organisation has called on the Swazi government to honour the commitments on human rights under international law that it has signed up to, but nothing has been implemented. Just the opposite, in fact. The US did take away its AGOA status on 1st January 2015 for lack of progress in human rights which formed part of the rules for having this duty free trade agreement. This particularly concerned the textile industry, the third largest export market, mainly owned by Taiwanese. Swaziland is the last remaining African country to recognise Taiwan as a country in its own right and springs to their defence in the UN assembly. This flattery gets the king massive financial donations of millions of US dollars for private aeroplanes, an airport, conference centre, hundreds of computers, rebuilding part of the Mbabane hospital, thousands of sneakers for the Reed Dance participants, rice for the starving and at least US$1.7 million towards the king's 50/50 birthday party. None of that is in the public domain, nor does it go down well with the public in Taiwan. In response, Taiwanese businessmen could take advantage of the US markets through the AGOA trade agreement.. However, they didn't hesitate to back out when the US withdrew it, which threw thousands, mostly women, out of work. These were mainly the sole breadwinners of their families and although the women's leaders crawled to the king on hands and knees, sang his praises, begged for his help and presented him with a white bull they could scarcely afford, they could not get him to budge an inch on human rights and so joined the ranks of the 40% unemployed that Swaziland already has. The agreement was reinstated 18 months later after the US elections.

South Africa also got turned down when the loan Swaziland asked for came with human rights strings attached. The UK has threatened expulsion from the Commonwealth and the EU, though still the biggest donor, has scaled down its help concentrating now on rural development, health and education. Fiscal reform urged by the IMF has been ignored. The Customs Union share it gets from SACU, though weighted very much in its favour, has also fallen since South Africa is experiencing economic problems of its own. How long this state of affairs can last before Swaziland becomes bankrupt is anyone's guess. What then? A satellite state of SA possibly? Many of the international businesses have been taken over by South Africans as a strategic move to protect their own industries and are run as their subsidiaries. "Swaziland, South Africa's willing captive" is already a phrase in general use. The ANC government could quite probably topple the Swazi monarchy but chooses not to. Only the S. African Trade Unions try to help their fellow workers in the kingdom. The King is not worried though. He's just acquired what amounts to a half share in the reopened Lufafa gold mine in the Hhohho region under the ownership of Jakop Arabo, an Uzbekh-American millionaire jeweller who was jailed in the US for 30 months for links to a drug ring, tax evasion and money laundering. Nevertheless, the King's share could be worth anything from US$ 67,000,000 to US$ 148,400,000 at present gold prices. Those circumstances might perhaps explain the gold dining set and lounge suite and the million dollar Jacob Arabo watches the king and some of the royal house are sporting.

 Some of his wives, meanwhile, together with an entourage of 100 have just spent US$1,000,000 on a holiday in Florida, while the US Ambassador is trying her best to persuade her government to donate US$1mill. of the US taxpayers' hard earned money for food relief. She has threatened to stop any more relief if the Swazi government is not prepared, at least, to donate an equal amount of money to save the lives of its own citizens. She is not the only diplomat who is uneasy at having to account to their governments for these aid packages in the face of extravagant royal spending, but the prospect of children dying seems to mean more to the international community than it does to the royal house. It does leave Aid Agencies with a dilemma. Take the example of the EU paying to start up free primary education and meals in 300 schools in 2010 for grade one pupils for five years after which the Swazi government should have taken over. It was extended for a further two years to give the government more time to get its act together, but it came to an end in 2018. The government was then left with a dilemma. It was short of money so which was it to be? A gold lounge suite for the king's 50/50 celebrations, a $30 million jet plane, a fifty tier birthday cake, 700 guests, millions in donations, a coat studded with diamonds or children's food and education? I doubt there was even a choice. As long as Aid Agencies and foreign governments are persuaded to foot the bill, Swazi government money will end up in the royal coffers.

The only corporation which has not granted the King a share is Coca Cola. The international giant moved over the border into Swaziland in 1987 to avoid the sanctions imposed on the Republic and the voices of protest in the US. They were also able to benefit from the low business rate of 6.7% granted to them instead of the usual 27.5%. Swaziland had also outlawed trade unions, wages were low and there was a plentiful supply of sugar from the plantations in the Lowveldt. Those benefits more than compensated for the transport difficulties they had getting their sugar concentrate to markets all over Africa, Asia, New Zealand and Australia. Coca Cola accounts for 40% of Swazi GPD so in 2015 when the king asked for a 10% stake, they only had to threaten to leave and the "request" was withdrawn. Coca Cola helps to keep the royal family in power and the country from economic disaster; the Coca Cola kingdom. As Wanda Mkhonsa states,

"We have this regime not because it is doing well but because the businesses around it are doing well." Which is probably why the firm gives the royal family an annual freebie holiday to Coca Cola HQ in Atlanta every year.

The King's plane showing the interior modifications.

Bread and circuses

To counter criticism from the international community, the royal house points to the popularity of its two major festivals as evidence that the people of Swaziland are united and happy with the governance it has now. They have the conviction that the traditional ceremonies of the Umhlanga, (the Reed Dance) and the Incwala (first fruits) which is used to sanctify the Kingship, demonstrate that the people are united behind their King. As Matsebula points out, variations of the incwala are celebrated by a number of ethnic groups in Southern Africa under another name as part of Nguni tradition: umkhosi for the Zulus; ioma for the Sotho; ingxwala for the Mpondo and so on. It was a very important ceremony when people depended on their harvests for survival. It was seen as unifying the tribe in thanking the ancestors for a good harvest and invoking their blessing for the well being of the tribe as embodied in their leaders, in the year to come. In Swaziland this ceremony is far more elaborate. It's the high point of the year; a sacred celebration of national identity and since it is the only Nguni nation with a population in thrall to the King, his participation has to take centre stage and when there is no King, as during his minority, there is no incwala.

It consists of a small and great Incwala covering a period of several weeks at harvest time in December and January depending on the phases of the moon and the dictates of the royal astronomers. The whole country winds down and it's seen as a time for reflection on their identity and a corporate prayer to the ancestors. There is a gathering of all the age regiments from young boys to old veterans in full regalia hung about with cows' tails and animal skins and head feathers, carrying shields and staffs and incorporating ritual, magic, liberal use of special herbs and narcotic muti, singing and dancing, killing a black bull and certain sexual activities which are kept hidden from the public in an inner sanctum. All of which serve to cleanse the King of all disagreeable and evil things by putting them on others while he is left clean and untouchable.

There are tasks allotted to certain age groups or ranks such as making a pilgrimage some 200 km on foot to the seashore south of Maputo with a sacred calabash to collect sea water as part of the cleansing ritual. This might also be a tribute to the historic journey of the Dlamini clan in the C18 from there to their present home in Swaziland. Particular clans are allotted the task of collecting special branches to form the walls of the sacred enclosure when the King goes into secret seclusion. While other young warriors, who are said to be sexual virgins, go to gather water from a certain river. Groomed by older veterans on the way, they learn the traditions of the

Swazi and swear oaths of allegiance to the king. Not only is the Incwala a reaffirmation of the monarchy, it is also a means of reinforcing the dominance of the Dlamini clan since some chiefs of other clans are not allowed to attend and there is strong emphasis on the rank and status of certain families delineating what tasks they are allowed to do in the rituals. Much emphasis is placed on the dancing of the age regiments, which can last hours at a time and singing songs exclusive to the ceremony.

After the King has tasted the first fruits of the harvest and given permission for the people to do the same, the main events are over and clearing up time involves a huge fire burning everything that has been used. The Queen Mother is supposed to use her rain making powers to bring on the rain to douse the flames and this used to work beautifully in years gone by before climate change. You could almost set your watch by the start of the monsoon rains, but that is no longer the case. When the magic fails, outside evil forces have to be blamed. Then it only remains for the age regiments to weed the maize fields of the King, the Queen Mother, all the King's wives and then the Chiefs. No small task. This feudal, unpaid tribute labour is described by Trade Unionists as slave labour but if it isn't done, fines are imposed. In 2015 the opening of schools was postponed for a week so the children could finish the weeding the fields of the King, the royal family members and the Chiefs! The latter too are under pressure to provide good participation at royal functions or they have to explain themselves to the royal overseers and, although the position of Chief has been hereditary, the King has ousted several of them recently in favour of his family members.

The celebration of the Swazi incwala leaves both the Christians and the modernizers with a dilemma. While they are justly proud to be Swazis, the Christians see some of the ceremonies, as described by Sithembiso Simelane, Hebron Dlovu and others, as un-Christian or positively evil examples of witchcraft. They particularly abhor the narcotics, the drugging of the King, his sodomizing the bull and the sexual intercourse with the two official wives witnessed by the group of King-makers to check his manhood which is supposed to cleanse the King by transferring all the evil onto the wives. That is their main function. Although they have petitioned in vain for certain alterations of the ceremony, many Christians do nevertheless attend, both because it is a celebration of their identity and because they fear for their career prospects if they don't. The pro democracy lobby see it as cementing the status quo which they are so opposed to and an endorsement of the King's position and power, so many keep away. But again, it is a celebration of their nationhood,

235

wholly paid for by Tibiyo taka Ngwane which is, after all, supposed to be there for the benefit of the nation. There's also plenty of roast meat and home brewed beer freely available for the undernourished and hungry and the Swazis do love to party!

If any Swazi woman is caught walking around town or on a bus wearing shorts, a mini skirt, trousers or a tank top even, she is liable to a fine, a beating, or get herself arrested by the local Chief or his henchmen. In 2010 the Chief of Lwandle in Manzini publicly stripped a woman naked for wearing trousers in his territory. Apart from the being briefly reported in The Times of Swaziland, no further action was taken. Nor is it an isolated incident. MPs also seem to spend more time debating how women should be allowed to dress, quoting a 19th century law on "immoral dressing", than they do on the parlous state of the economy. However, if any family refuses to send their teenage daughter to the Umhlanga ceremony for a week to parade almost naked all day before thousands of onlookers, they are liable to a fine and punishment could include the girl forfeiting a scholarship.

When Sobhuza revived the graded age regiments as part of his retribalization, he did the same for the girls and in 1940 he revived the Umhlanga, the reed dance, which was the traditional celebration of Swazi pre marital womanhood where the country's virgins come together for eight days in late August to pay tribute to the Queen Mother, show their loyalty to the King in song and dance and provide tribute labour to the Queen Mother by the gathering of special large reeds to renew the windbreaks around the Ndlovukasi's residence. It was meant to be a way of disciplining the young women and, at first, there were strict rules laid down about chastity, signified by the umqwasho, (coloured woolen halter) and when the girls were allowed to marry. That tradition faded and neither was the reed dance held every year until after Mswati's coronation when its tourist potential was recognized. It is now the country's biggest annual tourist attraction and almost a referendum on the King's reign to show the world, he says, how much his people love him, with endless anti democracy songs driving home the message.

The Chiefs are responsible for bringing the young girls in their district to the Reed Dance, usually packed, standing up, in the back of open lorries, or at least they did before the tragedy in 2015 when an accident occurred during umhlanga. An overloaded lorry some of the girls were travelling in collided with the back of another vehicle and many of the girls were killed, thrown into the path of oncoming traffic. When the king heard the news he didn't announce the fact or offer his condolences. Instead, he opted to carry on and not to alter celebrations in any way. He ordered a news blackout and forbade photography or journalists reporting how many were killed or injured, which vary to date from 13 to 63. Calls for a postponement of the ceremony or for a public announcement were dismissed. Hush it all up. Nothing must disturb the biggest tourist attraction of the year.

A similar reaction occurred when his 12th wife, the beautiful Senteni Masango took her own life following abuse allegations just before his 50/50 birthday celebrations in 2018. Keep it as quiet as possible.

Later on MP Gundwane Gamedze justified the joint burial of the lorry accident victims as "Cost effective" and called them "troops of the monarch, who, by being buried together would be appreciated as heroes dying for their King." But he didn't say how many were put into the joint grave.

Sometimes the King choses a glamorous new wife during the Reed Dance ceremonies, having looked again at the proceedings on tape to see what's on offer; who takes his fancy. Certainly almost nothing is left to the imagination, with just a beaded short pelmet or skirt to cover their pubic hair and nowadays the reintroduction of woolen umcwasho halters to herald their virgin status. Judging by the latest images, of which there are hundreds, the skirts seem just a tiny bit longer since my first and only visit to the Reed Dance, the buttocks not quite so visible and the dancing more tourist friendly, more managed and less of a huge crowd shuffle. What has also changed are the number of children taking part. This I find quite worrying given the uncontrolled tourist access to photographing. It's a pedophiles' paradise.

Most of the girls taking part seem to enjoy the experience. They're relieved of their household chores for a whole week, get together with their friends, the poor ones appreciate the pocket money they are paid and the meals they are given. There is some levelling down between aristocrats and commoners, though royalty is still distinguished by the red feathers in their hair, but they all dance together. They are proud of their own bodies and the fact that they are not among that large proportion of Swazi teen aged pregnancies where the highest incidence of AIDS is registered.

As Juvenal observed almost 2,000 years ago, "The powerful use 'bread and circuses' to distract and dupe the populace so they are sated and entertained instead of being politically engaged." It's sad to realise how little has changed.

In Zululand the Reed Dance was revived by King Goodwill Zwelithini in 1991 as part of cultural tourism and as a means, they say, of controlling AIDS in the region, the highest in the Republic. It is confined, (or supposed to be) to girls between 16 and 19 which King Goodwill took advantage of in choosing a new wife some 28 years younger than himself. It also aims, in various ways, to teach the young women about Aids, under age pregnancies, careers and the traditions of the Zulu nation. Like the Swazis, they are also topless and wear short beaded skirts but have the added indignity of having a physical examination by groups of elderly women to confirm their virginity and have their knickers confiscated if they try to wear them. Tradition dating back to the time of Shaka Zulu must be loyally adhered to, say the old women and besides, official confirmation of virginity adds to their value, and will command a better bride price. This practice has caused strong protests from among the women's groups of South Africa and quite how it is supposed to achieve the aim of lowering the incidence of AIDs is not altogether clear.

Finding pictures of some of the girls performing in the ceremony on pornographic websites has led to some re thinking, especially after some protests from US Baptist lobbies who donate a lot of money to Swaziland. Both Kings now have reservations about the very short beaded skirts and speak of replacing them with something a little longer (umutsha) so the girls can wear some underwear and not "expose their private parts" as they kick their legs up. Cultural tourism is not the only aim of onlookers.

What must have been an exciting celebration of a coming of age in the tribe, of the girls' pride in their purity and self worth in the time of Shaka 200 years ago now has to contend with politics, commercialism, political correctness, and all the other complex aspects of 21st century life. But alas, the freedom enjoyed by many of the world's women in the twenty-first century has left those in Swaziland behind. They have no rights and they have no voice but they are capable and resilient. Swaziland is of no importance to the rest of the world known now primarily for the obscene extravagance of its King with his diamond encrusted suit costing millions for his 50th birthday, his million dollar watches, gold dining room and his cars and jet planes. According to the Brookings Institution and Oxfam, Swaziland has the distinction of being the most unequal country in the world. His people are dependent on food aid, the children stunted, its women abused and life expectancy has dropped since Independence to a mere 48 years.. Either the world looks away or doesn't know what lies behind the smokescreen so we need to make the world aware. Swaziland is vanishing from the world's maps, from the world's consciousness but eSwatini must not be allowed to get away with this abuse of its women and children. What it is counting on is its secrecy, its anonymity. It fears the world knowing the truth; it fears being shamed; it fears losing its unwarranted reputation as a peaceful, happy land where the young women want nothing better than dancing and singing for their King, where the height of young men's ambition is to partake in the annual incwala ceremony.

The world needs to know the true state of affairs. The silent voices need to be heard.

Printed in Great Britain
by Amazon

66223978R00144